The Reflexology Healing Bible

Release your inner energy with
your fingertips to relieve pain,
reduce stress and promote healing

Denise Whichello Brown

Quantum
Books

A QUANTUM BOOK

Copyright © 2012 Quantum Publishing Ltd

All rights reserved. No part of this book may
be reproduced or translated in any form or
by any means without the written
permission of the publisher, except for the
inclusion of brief quotations in review.

ISBN: 978-1-84573-514-2

Produced by
Quantum Publishing Ltd
The Old Brewery
6 Blundell Street
London N7 9BH

QUMTRXB

Assistant Editor: Jo Morley
Editor: Jo Godfrey Wood
Managing Editor: Samantha Warrington
Production Manager: Rohana Yusof
Publisher: Sarah Bloxham

Packaged by Gulmohur

Printed in China by Midas Printing
International Ltd.

Quantum would like to thank and
acknowledge the following for supplying the
pictures reproduced in this book:

Shutterstock: 12, 59, 62, 68, 72, 75, 85, 86,
96, 108, 110, 114, 122, 126,
130, 132, 134, 149, 165, 188
iStock: 112, 118, 120, 124, 146, 153,
196, 208

All other photographs and illustrations are
the copyright of Quantum Publishing Ltd

While every effort has been made to
credit contributors, Quantum would like
to apologize should there have been any
omissions or errors.

The material in this book originally appeared
in *Reflexology A Practical Introduction* and
Hand Reflexology A Practical Introduction.

Contents

Origins and Principles of Reflexology

Reflexology is a simple, non-invasive, harmless and natural way to achieve optimum health. Firm pressure is applied through the thumbs and fingers to reflex points which are located on all parts of the hands and feet. By applying pressure on these points, all the organs, glands and structures of the body can be stimulated and encouraged to heal.

Reflexology is an ancient therapeutic treatment for activating the innate healing powers of the body. Ancient techniques of pressure have been practised for thousands of years by many different cultures. It is widely thought, although never proven, that reflexology has its origins in China more than 5,000 years ago. However, the first evidence depicting the practice comes from Egypt. In Saqqara, in the tomb of Ankmahor, an Egyptian physician, an ancient painting which dates back to around 2330 BC depicts treatments of the hands and feet actually taking place (see opposite page). The hieroglyphics are as follows:

'Do not let it be painful.' (patient)
'I shall act so you praise me.'
(practitioner)

Our modern concepts of reflexology originated with the zone therapy of the American physician Dr William Fitzgerald (1872–1942). Born in Connecticut, he graduated from the University of Vermont in 1895 and practised at Boston City Hospital, the Central London Ear Nose and Throat (E.N.T.) Hospital and also in Vienna. Dr Fitzgerald became the head physician in the ear, nose and throat department at St. Francis's Hospital, Connecticut and it was from here that he made the medical profession aware of his 'zone therapy'. Dr Fitzgerald discovered that if pressure was applied to specific areas or points on the body an anaesthetic effect could be induced. Not only could pain be relieved, but also the conditions producing the pain.

In 1917 Dr Fitzgerald, together with his colleague Dr Edwin Bowers, published a book entitled *Zone Therapy, Relieving Pain at Home*, and devised a dramatic demonstration for convincing sceptics of the theory's validity. First they applied pressure to a volunteer's hand, then stuck a pin into the anaesthetised area of the person's face – with no apparent pain.

Left Illustration from Ankmahor's tomb in Saqqara, Egypt. Dated around 2330 BC.

7

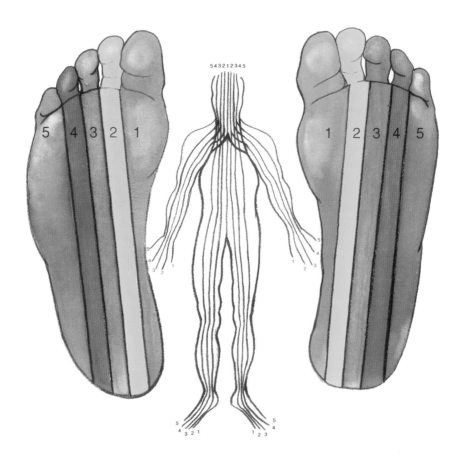

Above The ten longitudinal zones of the body and how they correspond to the zones on the feet.

In this book, Dr Fitzgerald divided the body into ten longitudinal zones of equal width running the length of the body, from the tips of the toes to the head and out to the fingertips and vice versa. He claimed that if a line is drawn through the centre of the body there are five zones to the right of this mid-line and five zones to the left of it. Zone one runs from the big toe, up the leg and centre of the body to the head and then down to the thumb. Zone two runs from the second toe, up to the head and down to the index finger. Zone three extends from the third toe, up to the head, down to the third finger and so on. All organs and parts of the body lie along one or more of these zones. Stimulating any part of a zone in the foot by applying direct pressure affects the entire zone throughout the body.

Dr Fitzgerald's theories began to spread across America. Although many in the medical profession were sceptical about his work, Dr Joseph Shelby-Riley, a chiropractor, was a true believer. Fitzgerald taught zone therapy to Shelby-Riley and his wife Elizabeth, who were both keen practitioners. Dr Shelby-Riley wrote several books including *Zone Therapy Simplified* (1919). He is renowned for introducing Eunice Ingham, a physiotherapist, to zone therapy.

Eunice Ingham (1879–1974) is considered to be the founder and mother of modern reflexology. It was through her work that foot reflexology was born in the early 1930s. In 1938 she published *Stories the Feet Can Tell*, followed by the sequel *Stories the Feet Have Told*. These classic texts are still used by reflexologists today.

She mapped out the entire body on the feet, which she viewed as being a mirror, or a mini-map, of the body. When Eunice retired in the 1970s after dedicating her life to reflexology, her work was continued by her nephew Dwight Byers.

Reflexology was introduced into Britain in the 1960s by Doreen Bayley (1900–1979) who had trained with Eunice Ingham.

Apart from the longitudinal zones, the feet can also be divided into transverse or horizontal sections. Transverse zones were first described by the German reflexologist, Hanne Marquart, who also trained with Eunice Ingham. The four transverse lines are as follows:

A. The shoulder girdle line located just below the base of the toes.
B. The diaphragm line located just below the ball of the foot.
C. The waist line in the middle of the foot in the centre of the arch of the foot.
D. The pelvic line just above the heel.

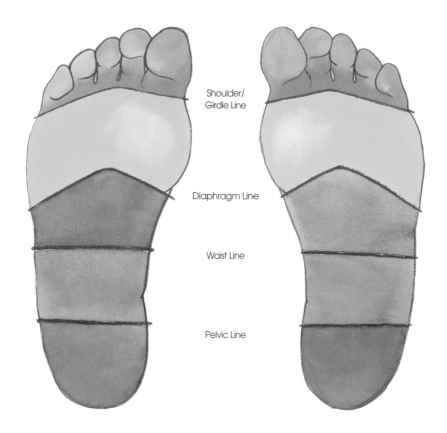

Shoulder/
Girdle Line

Diaphragm Line

Waist Line

Pelvic Line

Above The four transverse zones.

Opposite The feet mirror the body.

These imaginary lines help us to map out the body on the feet. All the organs and structures of the head and neck lie above the first transverse zone – the shoulder girdle line.

All organs above the diaphragm on the body will be represented above the diaphragm line on the foot. All organs below the diaphragm are found below the diaphragm line on the foot.

The feet precisely mirror the body. The right foot corresponds to the right-hand side of the body, while the left foot reflects the left-hand side. Paired organs such as the lungs, kidneys or ovaries are found one in each foot. Single organs such as the liver or spleen are found either in the right or the left foot according to where they are located in the body.

The spine, which is in the centre of the body, is found in both feet along the inside (medial aspect) of the foot. Outer parts of the body such as the shoulders, knees and hips are found on the outside (lateral aspect) of the foot.

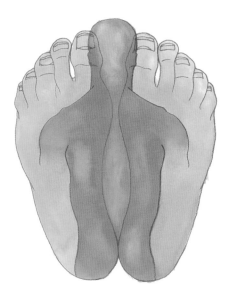

Checklist

- Reflexology should NEVER be used to diagnose medical conditions. A medical diagnosis should only be carried out by a qualified doctor.
- When giving a reflexology treatmen, you must NEVER promise to 'cure' an ailment, nor should you use reflexology to give false hope. However, everyone WILL benefit from reflexology.
- Reflexology should NOT be used instead of orthodox medicine. The advice of a medically qualified doctor should always be sought. However, reflexology and orthodox medicine work well when used together.
- Reflexology should NOT be classed as a medical treatment.
- Reflexology is NOT like an acupuncture treatment. Acupuncturists talk about 'meridians' whereas reflexologists use 'zones'. Acupuncture is an extremely complex subject, which can take four years of full-time study to qualify in. It can be very dangerous if not practised properly.

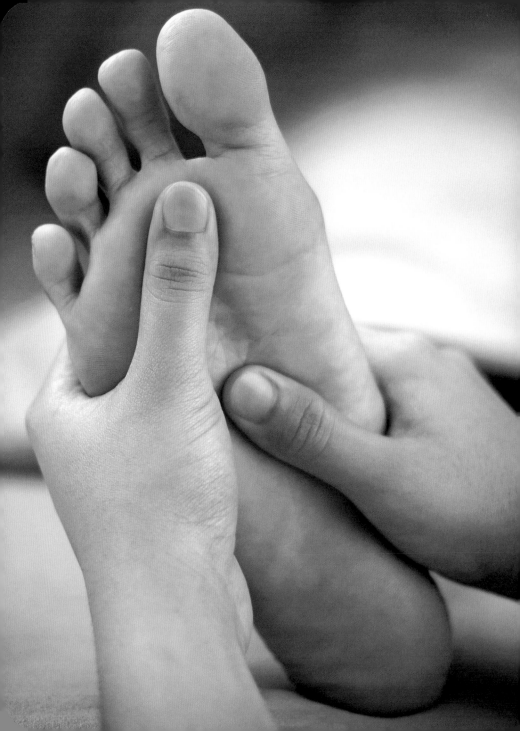

Foot Reflexology

This section details everything you need to know about treating the reflex points on the feet, including the various techniques you will need to learn in order to bring about healing in the whole body.

Introduction to Reflexology

Reflexology is a simple, non-invasive, harmless and natural way to achieve optimum health. It is easy to perform and no special equipment is required in order to practise it.

Above Pressure applied to areas on the feet can influence corresponding regions of the body. This simple movement encourages the spine to relax.

Reflexology is simple and effective – all you need are your hands and a willing partner or client. Firm pressure is applied through the thumbs and fingers to reflex points which are located on all parts of the feet. By applying pressure on these points, all the organs, glands and structures of the body can be stimulated and encouraged to heal. This book will enable the complete beginner to soothe away the stresses and strains of everyday life and promote well-being. It will also allow you to alleviate a whole host of common conditions such as headaches, backache, digestive problems, menstrual problems, arthritis, coughs and colds, insomnia and many more. It is important to realise, however, that reflexology should not be used instead of orthodox medical treatment – if problems persist then medical advice should be sought. Reflexology must also never be used to diagnose illness. Diagnosis is the prerogative of a doctor.

Reflexology has enormous physiological and psychological benefits on all the systems of the body.

Reflexology Induces Relaxation

Stress is a part of our everyday life and if we do not manage it properly then the body's defences break down, making us more susceptible to illness. It is generally conceded that 75 percent to

80 percent of ailments are attributed to stress and reflexology is capable of inducing a state of deep relaxation and tranquillity. The alpha state of relaxation is generated during a treatment, which leads to a level of consciousness at which healing can take place. During a reflexology session most people tend to fall asleep and awake refreshed and restored with a wonderful sense of well-being and inner harmony.

Reflexology is Preventative Health Care

Reflexology boosts the immune system and thus prevents illnesses and diseases from occurring. As the reflex zones on the feet are treated, the natural healing forces within the body are released and mobilised, restoring the body to harmony. Since the time of Hippocrates, health has been defined as a balanced state and disease as an unbalanced state or 'dis-ease'. Instead of passively waiting for the harmony to fall into disorder, which allows health problems to develop, reflexology aims to achieve this homeostasis. Patients who receive regular reflexology treatments report that they are far less susceptible to catching colds and flu even though everyone around them may be coughing and sneezing. Reflexology has effectively strengthened their immunological defences and thus enhanced their health.

Left Calming accessories can aid relaxation.

15

Reflexology Improves the Circulation

It is vital for blood to flow freely throughout the body as it carries essential oxygen and nutrients to the cells. Circulation can become sluggish and the blood flow can be restricted and impeded. Reflexology can improve the blood flow to every part of the body.

Reflexology Detoxifies the Body

The lymphatic system and the systems of elimination such as the colon, kidneys and skin are responsible for the detoxification of the body. If they are not functioning properly then toxins will build up. These waste deposits, which are similar to minute grains of sugar, can be palpated by sensitive fingers on the reflex zones of the feet and can be broken down by reflexology massage and eliminated.

Below A reflexology treatment is so relaxing that the patient often falls asleep.

Reflexology Revitalises Energy

Reflexology regenerates and opens up energy pathways, revitalising the body and supplying it with renewed and invigorating energy. We are all very much aware of when our 'batteries' are low and many

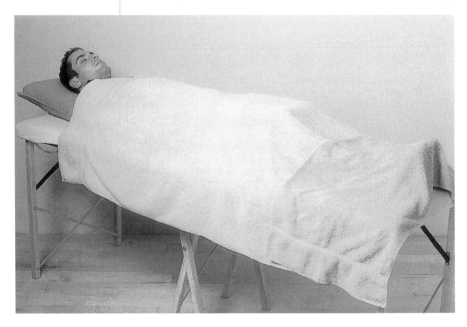

individuals feel tired and lethargic all the time. It is vital that we recharge our batteries with reflexology as often as we are able.

Reflexology Improves Mental Function

Reflexology calms the mind and relieves it of all unnecessary 'clutter'. Thus mental alertness is restored, thoughts can be clarified and new ideas can be stimulated.

Reflexology Stimulates Emotional Release

Reflexology can adjust emotional imbalances in the body. During treatments, unresolved emotional problems are encouraged to rise to the surface and can then be dealt with. Many physical ailments stem from an emotional source. Negative states of mind will block the free flow of the life force and cause disease. As the old, unwanted emotions are released, changes in attitude and personality often take place and balanced health is restored.

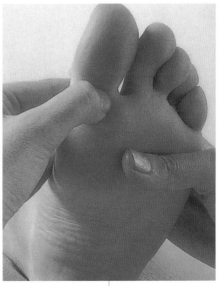

Above Toxins can be identified as small grains and broken down during a reflexology treatment.

17

Getting Started

It is important to create a relaxing environment for treating reflexology clients. There are many simple things you can do to transform your treatment area in order to maximise calm and healing.

Creating the Right Ambience

Reflexology does not require any complicated or expensive equipment. All you need are your hands, your intuition and the desire to help others. Although reflexology can be performed almost anywhere, it is well worth creating the right environment to allow the recipient to derive maximum benefit from a treatment.

The surroundings should be as peaceful as possible. As the aim of your treatment is to induce relaxation, the noise of telephones ringing, children or traffic will not help to create a healing atmosphere. Put all phones on 'silent' setting and make sure that your family know that you are carrying out a treatment. Some people will enjoy listening to relaxation music in the background during their reflexology treatment, while others will prefer silence to help them relax. It is entirely up to individual preference.

Setting Out Your Room

Below Fresh flowers help to create a relaxing environment.

The treatment room should be very warm and inviting. Although only shoes and socks are removed, some loss of body heat is inevitable as the treatment progresses. Warmth will encourage feelings of security and relaxation. Lighting should be soft and subdued. Bright lights should be dimmed or even switched off and replaced with candles. Tinted bulbs can also provide the perfect setting. You may wish to burn some essential oils or incense prior to your treatment or have a vase of fresh flowers in the room to add to the friendly, relaxed atmosphere.

Small clay burners for diffusing essential oils are readily available and reasonably priced. Put a few teaspoonsful of water into the bowl on the top and sprinkle a few drops of your chosen essential oil into it. Light the tea light and allow the wonderful aromas to diffuse into the atmosphere. Suitable essential oils for creating an atmosphere of relaxation include lavender, clary sage, geranium, jasmine, neroli, ylang-ylang or rose.

Positions for Working

A professional reflexologist will use a massage couch, but it is not essential to buy one. You may decide to invest in one later on, but for home use a normal bed is all that you require. The receiver should lie down with his/her feet at the foot of the bed. Pillows should be placed under the head to support the neck and to allow you to observe any facial expressions. You may also wish to place a pillow under the receiver's knees to take any pressure off the lower back. A pillow or cushion placed under the foot that you are working on may be useful for your own comfort. It is important that you are just as relaxed as the receiver.

Position yourself on a swivel chair or a stool in a relaxed upright posture. Make sure that your back and shoulders are not strained or tense. Your legs and knees should be slightly apart, your feet on the ground and your shoulders should be down and relaxed. If there is any tension in your body then the receiver will almost certainly be aware of it. If your hands are tense they will not move smoothly and they will be unable to feel any abnormal reflex areas in the feet.

Above A few drops of soothing aromatic oil in a burner provide a soothing atmosphere.

Far Left Place a pillow under the receiver's knees for added comfort.

Left It is important to sit with a correct posture in order to perform reflexology effectively.

19

Above If a couch or
bed is unavailable,
reflexology can be
easily practised on
the floor.

You may prefer to work on the floor using a well-padded surface. Place a thick duvet, or two or three blankets, on the floor. Either kneel or sit cross-legged and rest the receiver's foot on your lap or on a pillow. You will still need pillows or cushions under the receiver's head and knees. Some people like to work with the receiver sitting on a chair, but this will not suit everyone. It is not as comfortable for either the giver or the receiver. It also seems to encourage conversation and it is important to keep talking to a minimum to achieve the best results. Relaxation is essential to allow energy from both of you to flow freely throughout the treatment.

A light blanket or towel should be used to cover up the receiver even though the clothes are not removed. As the treatment progresses there will be some loss of body heat.

Any restrictive clothing such as ties and belts should be removed to allow the energies to flow freely. You should also remove any jewellery such as rings and bracelets to avoid scratching. Ensure that your fingernails are closely clipped and smoothly filed to avoid any discomfort. Always remember to wash your hands both before and after a treatment.

Below Ensure your
hands are clean and
nails are clipped
smoothly before
beginning a
treatment. Remove
all jewellery.

Refreshing the Feet

You may wish to cleanse the feet prior to a reflexology session. Sweaty, unpleasant smelling feet can cause embarrassment to the receiver and are not pleasant to work on either. You may want to soak the feet for a few minutes in a bowl of warm water, or simply wipe them gently with moist cotton ball. Add a few drops of essential oil of lavender, tea

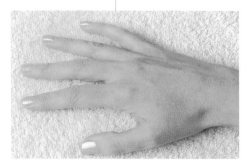

tree, lemon or peppermint to the water to relax and cleanse the feet. If you do not have any essential oils you may add a sprig of fresh lavender or peppermint from your garden, or squeeze some fresh lemon juice, into your bowl. Rosewater is excellent for cleansing the feet. However you decide to refresh the feet, always dry them thoroughly. Avoid using oils or creams during your treatment. Too much

Left Oils can be mixed to create an individual massage blend to be used at the end of the treatment.

lubricant will make it difficult for you to hold the foot properly and will cause your walking thumb or finger to slip. A barrier will also be created, decreasing your sensitivity and making it difficult for you to detect any abnormalities. Some people use talcum powder on the feet, but this can be messy and may block up the pores. It can also cause problems if it is inhaled accidentally.

Essential oils should never be applied undiluted to the skin. To make up a suitable massage blend, just add three drops of essential oil to two teaspoonfuls of a cold-pressed, unrefined, additive-free carrier oil such as sweet almond or apricot kernel. You may prefer to add your essential oils to a pure, organic skin cream in the same dilution. Add up to nine drops of an essential oil to a 28 g (l oz) glass jar to create an excellent foot cream.

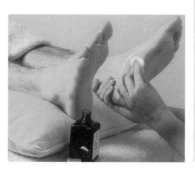

Left Rosewater is ideal for cleansing the feet.

Checklist

• These reactions NEVER occur simultaneously. After a treatment one or two reactions MAY occur.

Reactions from Reflexology

Both during and after a reflexology treatment, physical and psychological changes may occur. All responses should be seen as positive and highly desirable as reactions show that the body's self-healing mechanism is being activated. The body is trying to expel unwanted toxins. Reactions have been divided into those which may occur during a treatment and those which may appear between treatments.

Possible reactions during a treatment

• Changes in expression.
• Visible contraction of the muscles e.g. shoulders.
• A feeling of deep relaxation and the desire to sleep.
• A warm glow as energy blockages are released.
• Feelings of euphoria.
• Sensations of the body expanding and spreading as it relaxes.
• Shooting sensations as blockages release.
• Running nose if the head zones are being treated and are blocked.
• Twitching or tingling.
• Warmth in the area of the body being worked on.

Possible reactions between treatments

• A state of deep relaxation.
• An alteration in sleep patterns eventually leading to deep sleep.
• More frequent and noticeable dreams.
• Emotional changes with a greater awareness of feelings.
• Increased skin activity – pimples, rashes, increased perspiration. Eventually skin tone and texture improves.
• Increase in urination.
• Cloudy or unpleasant-smelling urine.
• Bowels move more frequently.
• Increase in bulk and volume of the stools.
• Nasal discharges.
• Coughing and secretions from the bronchi.
• Colds.
• Sneezing.

- Watery eyes.
- Sore throat.
- Fever.
- Vaginal discharges.
- Toothache.
- A need to drink more water to flush away the toxins.
- Previous illnesses which have been suppressed may flare up temporarily and then disappear.

Contraindications to Reflexology

Never use reflexology in these circumstances:
- Immediately after surgery until the doctor has pronounced complete recovery.
- When the receiver is suffering from a fever – the body is already fighting off toxins and a reflexology treatment would release more toxins into the system.
- If the receiver has an infectious skin conditions such as scabies as you do not want to spread the condition or infect yourself. NB: Conditions such as eczema and psoriasis are NOT infectious and should improve with treatment.
- If the receiver suffers from thrombosis – reflexology could move a clot.
- During pregnancy where there is an element of risk, especially during the first 12–14 weeks or if the pregnancy is complicated.

Basic Reflexology Techniques

As a beginner it is always useful to remember that everyone is different and some people will be more sensitive than others when it comes to being treated.

Checklist
- Do not grip the foot too tightly.
- Ensure your nails are trimmed.

Reflexology should NEVER be painful. Your pressure should be firm but not uncomfortable. If the receiver flinches or tries to withdraw his or her feet then you are pressing too hard. Every individual's feet will be different – some are much more sensitive than others. As you work, use your intuition and watch the facial expressions of the person receiving treatment. Adjust your pressure accordingly.

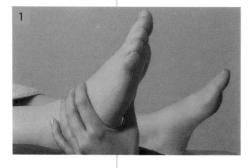

Holding Technique

To be a good reflexologist it is important to hold the foot correctly so that the reflex zones can be easily reached, accurately pinpointed and stimulated. You need to develop good teamwork between your hands as you will always be holding and working the foot with both of them. One hand is used to support and hold while the other hand will work the reflexes. To work on the right foot (see image 1) place the heel of your left hand against the outer aspect of the foot. Wrap the fingers of your left hand lightly over the front of the foot and the thumb under the sole. Reverse this for the left. foot. (see image 2).

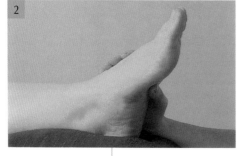

This position allows you to support and control the movement of the foot very effectively. The foot can be pushed backwards away from you, brought toward you or even twisted slightly. Practise this holding technique on the left foot too. This time your right hand will act as the holding hand, leaving your left hand free to work on the reflexes.

Thumb-Walking Technique

This movement is performed with the outer edge of the thumb.

To find this point place your hand palm downward on a flat surface and notice the tip of the thumb that touches the surface of the table – this outside tip is to be the working area of your thumb.

Strength in reflexology is made possible by the appropriate use of leverage, and leverage is achieved by the use of the four fingers in opposition to the thumb. First of all practise the caterpillar-walking on the palm of your hand or on your forearm.

To walk the thumb bend ONLY the first joint of the thumb slightly and then unbend it slightly. Only allow the thumb to take very SMALL steps as it walks along the hand/forearm. The walking

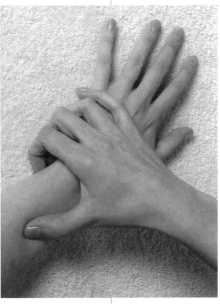

movement is always performed forward, never backwards or sideways. You should aim to maintain a constant, steady and even pressure. An on-off-on-off pressure should not be felt at each bend of the thumb. Do not worry if your thumbs start to ache or feel sore at first. With practice your thumbs will increase in tolerance and build up strength. Do not be discouraged – be patient and keep trying. As the thumb is walking, the four fingers should be moulded to the contours of the hand/forearm. The four fingers should be kept together comfortably to ensure maximum leverage. If they are spread out then some of the leverage will be lost.

Above Maintaining constant, even pressure, gradually 'walk' your thumb up the side of your wrist. Always move forward, not backwards or sideways.

25

Thumb-walking Technique Continued...

1. Practise thumb-walking up each of the five zones along the entire length of the foot.

2. Ensure that you are holding the foot correctly, with your supporting hand wrapped around the toes.

Checklist

- Ensure that you are holding the foot properly.
- Use the outer edge of the thumb.
- Do not dig your nail into the skin.
- Bend only the first joint of the thumb slightly.
- Employ a constant, steady pressure, NOT an on-off-on-off pressure.
- The thumb always moves forward, never backwards or sideways.

3. Work from the base of the heel in zone five up toward the base of the little toe.

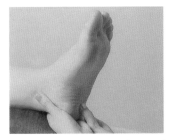

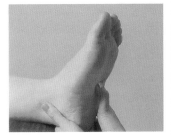

4. Now work from the base of the heel in zone four up toward toe four.

5. Repeat this thumb-walking up each of the other zones.

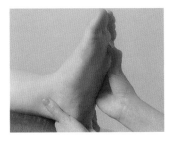

6. Then walk up each of the five zones on the other foot.

Below Use the first joint of your index finger to carry out finger-walking effectively.

Finger-walking

The finger-walking technique is basically the same as the thumb-walking technique. The first joint of the index finger is used.

Excellent places to practise your finger-walking are on the back of your hand or on your forearm. Use the corner edge of your index finger as you walk forward taking the smallest 'steps' possible while exerting a constant, steady pressure. Leverage is obtained by the use of the thumb in opposition to the fingers.

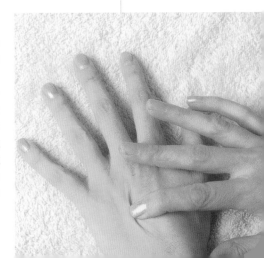

Finger-walking Technique Continued...

1. Any finger may perform this technique. Try it out on the receiver's foot. Usually only one finger is used at any one time.

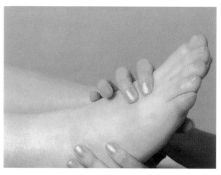

2. However, two or more fingers may sometimes be used, for example when working across the top of the foot.

Checklist

- Take only very small steps to cover the area.
- Always move your index finger forward, not backwards or sideways.
- Use the flat pad part of the outside edge of your thumb.

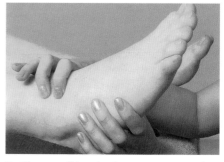

3. Finger-walking is the most appropriate technique when working on bony and sensitive areas such as the top of the foot and around the ankle, as shown here.

28

Hook-in and Back-up

This technique is used to apply pressure to specific points and it requires great accuracy. Certain points on the feet are either too small or too deep for the walking techniques to be used effectively. However, this very precise technique should never be employed when covering a large area. It is ideal for contacting the tiny reflex points such as the pituitary gland, which is found on the big toe.

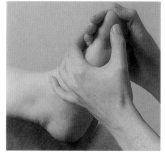

1. Place the thumb of your working hand onto your chosen reflex point. Apply pressure with your thumb.

2. Now pull back across the point with the thumb. Push in, then back up. You may repeat this technique several times.

3–4. Your thumb lands on a small point and hooks-in and backs-up.

29

Pressure Circles on a Point

This technique is particularly recommended for working on tender reflexes or sensitive areas on the foot.

Hold the foot comfortably with one hand and place the flat pad part of the thumb of the other hand onto the tender area.

1. The solar plexus area is shown here. Press slowly into the area and circle your thumb gently over the area several times. After a few pressure circles any tenderness should have diminished.

2. The thumb is always used for this technique, apart from the uterus/prostate and ovary/testicle points, where the index or the third finger is used. Here the uterus area is shown.

Rotation on a Point

This technique may be used on any tender reflexes.

Support the foot comfortably with one hand and place the pad of the thumb of your other hand onto the relevant reflex point. With your holding hand, flex the foot slowly into the thumb.

Rotate the foot in a circular motion around the thumb. In the steps below the technique is performed on the kidney reflex.

Checklist

• Rotate the foot slowly with your holding hand to bring about maximum relaxation.

• Ensure that you are not digging in with your thumbnail.

• Do not allow your thumb to slip off the reflex point.

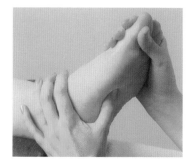

1. Flex the foot slowly into the thumb.

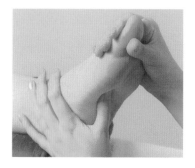

2. Rotate the foot around the thumb. Here, the technique is performed on the kidney reflex.

Reflexology Relaxation Techniques

Relaxation techniques are always used prior to a reflexology treatment. They are designed to put the receiver at ease and to help to establish a relationship of trust.

Checklist
- Don't use oils or creams for your preliminary relaxation sequence (although they may be used at the end of the treatment).
- Make sure that you remove rings, bracelets and watches before you start work.
- Check that your fingernails are short, smooth and even.

I f someone is having their feet worked on for the first time they are bound to feel a little nervous and may worry that the treatment will feel ticklish. These techniques will help to dispel any initial nervousness. They will also loosen any muscular tension in the feet and make them soft, supple and easy to work on.

Use these techniques in any order and repeat some of them throughout your reflexology treatment. It is not necessary to master all of them, so choose your favourites. As your confidence grows it is quite acceptable to create your own. Use a few relaxation techniques at the end of a complete treatment as a 'dessert' to enable the receiver to gain maximum benefit and pleasure.

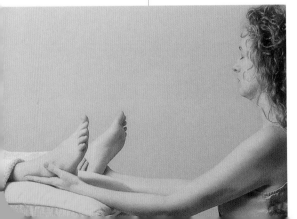

Tuning into the Feet
To begin the relaxation sequence, hold both feet. Take a few deep breaths, allowing all the tension to flow out of your body (see left).

As you tune into the person you are treating, imagine the healing energy flowing freely through your hands and body. You and the receiver should be completely relaxed.

Effleurage (Stroking)

1. Using both hands, stroke the whole foot firmly, covering both the top, the sides and the sole of the foot.

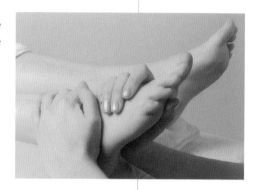

2. Work up from the toes, gliding around the ankle bones and back again.

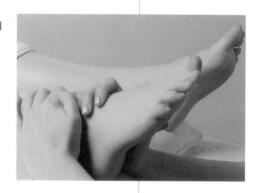

3. Repeat this movement several times. Stroking relaxes, increases blood flow and helps to disperse any excess fluid, especially around the ankles.

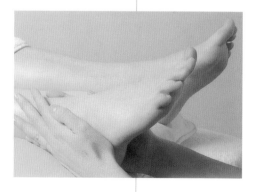

Metatarsal Kneading

The metatarsals are a group of five long bones in the feet, located between the tarsals and the toe phalanges. This kneading technique applied to this area helps to soften the tissues on the sole of the foot.

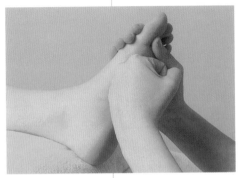

1. If working on the left foot, hold the top of it with your right hand just below the base of the toes. Your hand should 'wrap" around the foot, with your thumb on the sole and fingers on the top of the foot. Make a fist with the left hand and place it on the fleshy area on the ball of the foot

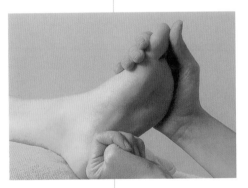

2. Work from the ball of the foot to the heel using a gentle circular motion.

Alternate Thumb Rotations

Thumb rotations are far more effective if you work your thumbs alternately. You will achieve an even coverage of the area and your hands and thumbs will not get so tired. Don't forget to treat both feet evenly.

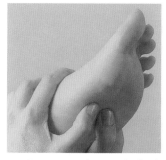

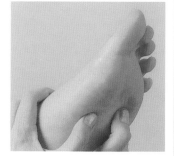

1. Grasp one foot with both hands so that your thumbs are on the bottom of the sole of the foot and your fingers are on the top.

2. Rotate one thumb at a time using small circular movements – alternate the right thumb clockwise and the left thumb anticlockwise.

3. Work up from the heel toward the toes.

Spreading the Foot

To achieve maximum effect, the foot being treated needs to be spread out as far as possible. Making a zigzag action is a helpful way to think of it. Repeat on the other foot.

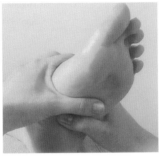

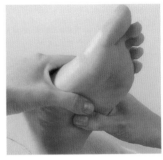

1. Hold the foot with both hands so that the balls of the thumbs are placed flat against the sole and the fingers are flat on top – one hand will be slightly higher than the other.

2. Pull the thumbs away and past each other, toward the edges of the foot, and then allow them to slide back toward each other.

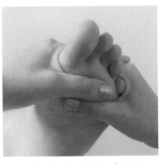

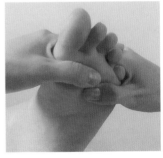

3. Work the thumbs in this zigzag movement from the base of the toes to the base of the heels and back again.

4. Feel that you are opening out the foot.

Spinal Stroking (Fanning the Spine)

This technique encourages the spine to relax and is excellent for neck and back-pain sufferers.

1. Cup the heel of one foot so that it is resting in the palm of your hand. This holding technique is first shown on the left foot to show the hand position clearly.

2. With the heel of the other hand, stroke firmly down the inside (medial aspect) of the foot, working from the big toe toward the heel. This movement is shown on the right foot.

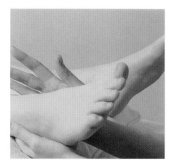

3. The inside edge of the foot corresponds to the spine.

Spinal Twist (Push and Pull)

Twisting the bottom of the foot loosens the lower back and working on either side of the ball of the foot loosens the upper back and alleviates stiffness in the shoulders.

1. Place one hand on the inside of the foot and the other on the outside. Using the heels of the hands, pull the outside of the foot toward you with one hand as you push the inside of the foot away from you and vice versa.

2. Work along the edges of the foot from the heel to the toes and back down again. Perform these movements slowly to further relax and improve mobility in the spine.

Toe Loosening

This technique will increase the flexibility of the toes and also loosen the muscles around the neck and shoulders.

1. Support the foot gently with one hand, thumb on the sole of the foot, and fingers wrapped around the top of the foot.

2. Using your thumb and index finger close to the base of each joint, gently stretch each toe.

3. Rotate each toe both clockwise and anticlockwise and repeat these steps.

Ankle Rotations

Ankle rotations stretch and loosen the foot muscles and improve circulation to the ankles. By rotating the foot in a complete circle you are providing both exercise and relaxation to the four major muscle groups that control the foot movements.

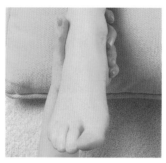 

1. Support the heel in one hand, thumb on the outside of the ankle, and fingers on the inside.

2. Grasp the top of the foot in your other hand and slowly and gently rotate the ankle several times in one direction and then in the other direction.

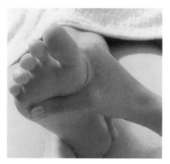

3. This movement helps relaxation and increases mobility in the lower back and pelvis.

Foot Rocking

This movement stimulates circulation and relaxes the muscles in the foot, ankle and calf.

1. Place the palms of your hands one either side of the foot.

2. Move them alternately and rapidly from side to side so that the foot vibrates.

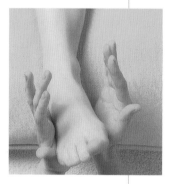

Lower Back Release

There are many things that can cause a dull ache in the lower back and it is particularly common in women who may experience a change in the centre of balance during pregnancy. Regular reflexology treatments can ease the pain and be a useful preventative measure.

1. Grasp underneath the heels of both feet.

2. Lean backwards and slowly and gently pull the feet toward you. Release the stretch just as slowly.

Diaphragm Release (Solar Plexus)

The solar plexus is the main area in the body which stores our stress and tension. Applying pressure to this area encourages a state of relaxation and also helps the breathing to deepen and slow down. This is the ultimate in relaxation techniques and it should always be used to complete a treatment. The solar plexus release may be performed on one or both feet.

You can synchronise this technique with the receiver's breathing. Ask them to take a deep breath and, as they do, press into the solar plexus. As they slowly breathe out you should release your pressure on the points.

1. To locate the solar plexus, place one hand over the top of the upper part of the foot and squeeze gently. A hollow will appear on the sole of the foot at the diaphragm line – this is the solar plexus. Release the foot, remembering where this point is. Now find the solar plexus on the other foot.

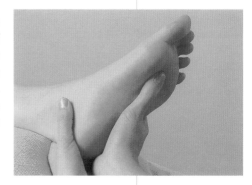

2. Take the left foot in your right hand and the right foot in your left hand, fingers on top, thumbs on the bottom. Place your thumbs onto the solar plexus reflex. Press the solar plexus reflex very gently and slowly. Hold for a few seconds. Release your pressure gradually, but do not lose contact with the feet. Do this several times.

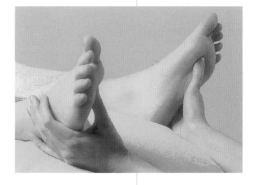

43

Beginning a Reflexology Treatment

Now that you have familiarised yourself with the basic techniques, and have also mastered some of the reflexology relaxation techniques, you are ready to work on the reflex points.

Remember that you should never diagnose conditions yourself – this is the prerogative of the medically qualified. Reflexology is not a substitute for orthodox medical treatment. If the receiver has a problem which does not resolve, then always tell them to seek the advice of a medically qualified doctor.

Length of Treatments

Below A complete treatment should last around 45 minutes, but individual needs may vary.

The timing of treatments and the amount of pressure used varies from individual to individual, depending upon their needs. A complete treatment with practice will probably take you about 45 minutes. For your initial treatment allow at least an hour. When working on a child, the younger the child the shorter the treatment. A baby would only need a five-minute treatment consisting of stroking movements, whereas an older child of 12 would be able to receive about 30 minutes. A treatment would also be shorter if you are working on elderly or very sick people. Reflexology is suitable for all ages and it is rare to find someone who will not benefit from treatment.

Do not be tempted to spend too long on a single treatment. If the session is too lengthy you may overstimulate the body. This could cause excessive elimination, resulting in diarrhoea or other uncomfortable conditions.

How Much Pressure to Use

It is important to work very gently during the first treatment session in order to see how the person reacts. The amount of pressure required will vary from one individual to another. If your partner feels as though he/she is being tickled then more pressure is needed. If the feet are jerked backwards away from you, then obviously you need to reduce the intensity of your treatment. Once you have established the right pressure you should sustain it evenly throughout the session.

It is interesting that a person will not necessarily always require the same amount of pressure. Factors such as emotional trauma or hormonal changes could well result in the feet becoming more sensitive. If the person is highly stressed or very debilitated then, again, light pressure should be used. Drugs such as painkillers or any medication that de-sensitises feeling will make the feet less sensitive.

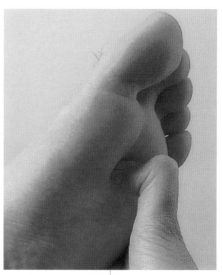

Above Applying excessive pressure can cause pain or discomfort.

As conditions improve you will probably find that you can use firmer pressure. However this does not mean that sensitive reflexes indicate an unhealthy person and insensitive reflexes indicate a healthy person. Some unhealthy people can have very insensitive reflexes, whereas some healthy people have very tender feet.

Always stroke the foot at frequent intervals throughout the treatment. This is not only very pleasant and relaxing but also will help to disperse any toxins that have been released.

What To Do if an Area is Painful

If you discover any tender reflexes on the feet you should only use GENTLE pressure over these areas for a short time. Treatment should NEVER be applied continuously over the same reflex point. It is far more effective (and comfortable) to return to any painful areas at frequent intervals and at the end of the treatment. Any uncomfortable areas should eventually disappear as health and balance are restored.

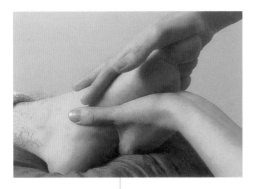

Number of Treatments

After the first treatment it is highly likely that an effect will be experienced. Most reactions are very pleasant but some minor irritations may be felt as the body rids itself of any toxins. Any adverse reaction should pass within 24 hours. For optimum results, and especially where there are minor ailments, you should try to treat the receiver once a week for approximately seven treatments. Carrying out a complete treatment more than once a week is not recommended as this could result in an area being over-stimulated. After the initial sessions, depending on how much time you have, once every two to four weeks is quite adequate.

If you want to pamper the receiver with more sessions it is quite acceptable to use the relaxation techniques as often as you like.

What a Treatment Feels Like

On the whole a treatment is extremely pleasurable for the receiver and very addictive. Most people will fall asleep during a session which is excellent for healing. However, the receiver may experience some strange sensations. Several people have reported feeling needle-like sensations, while others have experienced a dull ache in certain areas of the foot. Tingling sensations may also be felt as blockages are released. Overall, however, your receiver will feel incredibly relaxed and revitalised by the end of the session.

46

The Treatment

You are now ready to begin. Ask the receiver to lie on the bed or couch, make them warm and comfortable, and if necessary cleanse the feet. Check for any cuts, bruises, corns, verrucae or ingrowing toenails which could be tender or contagious. You will need to work gently on these areas or even avoid them altogether. Remember to always cover the foot you are not working on.

Opposite top Stroking feet regularly will relax the receiver, as well as dispersing toxins.

Opposite centre Check feet for tender areas before beginning treatment.

Personal Preparation

Before commencing your reflexology massage, it is important to prepare not only the environment and the receiver but also yourself. You need to centre yourself and clear your mind of all thoughts. Consciously release all tense areas of your body, particularly your neck, back and shoulders. To do this take a few deep breaths and, as you exhale, feel the tension melting away, leaving you relaxed and calm. As you breathe in draw in healing energy.

Opposite bottom Ensure that you are calm and relaxed before beginning a treatment.

Treatment Summary

The order of the sequence can be simplified as follows:

1. Relaxation techniques.
2. All toes – the head and neck area.
3. Inside of the foot – the spine.
4. Ball of the foot – the chest, breast, lungs, thyroid etc.
5. Arch/instep of the foot – the abdominal area containing organs such as the stomach, pancreas, intestines, kidneys etc.
6. Outside of the foot – joints such as the knee, hip, elbow etc.
7. Heel – the pelvic and leg reflexes.
8. Ankles – the reproductive area and lymphatics.
9. Relaxation techniques.

   Thus, you work each foot in a logical manner from the toes down to the heels.

Reflexology Sequence Right Foot

Now that you have learned all the basic foot techniques, try out a whole sequence on the right foot. In the following sequence (pp. 48-76) are all steps you will need, including the techniques to use and the order they should be carried out in.

Relaxation Technique

These techniques have already been described in detail in the previous chapter. Here only the basic movement for each technique is shown. Remember to always tune into the feet before beginning.

Effleurage/stroking p.33

Metatarsal kneading p.34

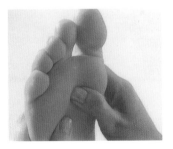

Alternate thumb rotations p.35

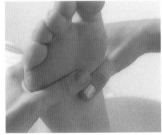

Spreading the foot p.36

Spinal stroking p.37

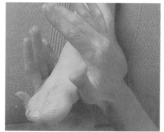

Spinal twist p.38

Toe loosening p.39

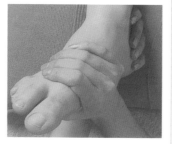

Ankle rotations p.40

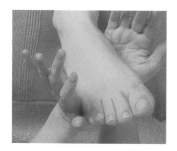

Foot rocking p.41

Tension Release

Diaphragm (Solar Plexus)

Stress can be caused by many different factors in life, but reflexology can be remarkably effective. It is a good idea to go slowly with the treatment and move the foot to help loosen it. Being too energetic in giving treatment may create further tension.

1. This is the primary area for the release of tension. To locate it, gently pull the toes backwards with your holding (left) hand to make the diaphragm line more visible. Place the fingers of the working hand on the top of the foot for leverage.

2. Thumb-walk across the diaphragm line, working from the medial aspect (inside) of the foot toward the outside.

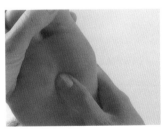

3. When you reach the solar plexus press gently into it as the recipient breathes in and release the pressure as the recipient breathes out. Repeat several times.

Head and Neck

Step 1 Head and Brain (Back and Sides of the Big Toe)

The head and neck area can store tension in the body and it is good to be able to release it. Reflexology techniques can be perfect for this. The reflex areas in the toes correspond to parts of the head and neck.

1. Place the heel of your left hand around the outer aspect of the foot. Wrap the fingers of your left hand over the front of the toes and your thumb under the back of the toes. Using your right thumb, walk from the outer edge of the base of the big toe up the outside, over the top and down the inside of the big toe.

2. Now walk up the back of the big toe from the base to the tip. You will probably need to walk up the big toe three to five times to cover the entire area. If you prefer you may walk down the big toe instead of up.

Step 2 Pituitary Gland (Big Toe)

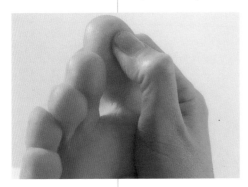

To find the pituitary gland reflex point, locate the widest point on each side of the big toe and imagine a line stretching across these points. The pituitary gland is found approximately at the mid-point of this line. You often have to search around to find this point. Place the fingers of your left hand over the front of the toes and your thumb under the back of the toes. With the corner of your right thumb use the hook-in and back-up technique on the pituitary gland reflex.

Step 3 Face (Front of the Big Toe)

Wrap your left hand around the top the foot, thumb underneath, fingers on top. Using your right index finger, walk down the front of the big toe from the tip of the big toe to the base. Caterpillar-walk down as many times as it is necessary to cover the whole of the front of the toe.

Step 4 Neck (Base of the Big Toe)

1. First of all of rotate the big toe. Support the foot with your left hand, hold the big toe between the thumb and index finger of your right hand and rotate it clockwise and anticlockwise. This is equivalent to rotation of the neck. Do this movement slowly and gently. If the toe grinds or cracks or is limited in movement as you move it, this indicates a problem with the neck.

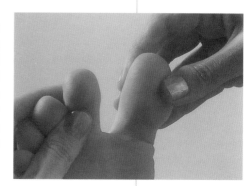

2. To loosen the neck further, gently grasp the big toe between the thumb and fingers of your left hand and with your right thumb-walk across the back of the base of the big toe from the outside to the inside to treat the back of the neck.

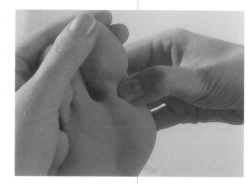

3. Now using your index finger, finger-walk across the front base of the big toe working from the outside to the inside.

Step 5 Sinuses (Back, Sides and Top of The Small Toes)

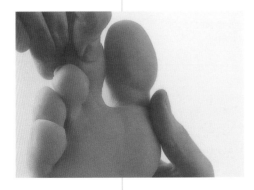

1. To work the sinuses you are going to walk down the centre and two sides of the small toes. Support the recipient's right foot between the thumb and fingers of your left hand – thumb on the sole of the foot, fingers over the front of the toes for support and control. Starting at the top of each toe using very small steps thumb-walk down to the base of each toe, or even both together.

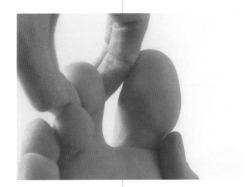

2. When treating the sides you may use your thumb or index finger, or both together. Do this movement three times, covering the centre and sides of each toe. You will probably find that working the sides of the toes is more difficult, but persevere. This technique can also be performed by working up the back and sides of the toes, instead of down.

Step 6 Teeth (Front of the Small Toes)

Starting at the base of the nail, walk down the fronts of the toes covering the centre of each toe and both sides of each toe from top to bottom.

Step 7 Upper Lymphatics (Between the Toes)

The reflex areas to the upper lymph nodes are found in the webbing between the toes. Support the foot with your left hand and, with the thumb and index finger of your right hand, very gently squeeze between each of the toes.

Step 8 Spine (Inner Edge of the Foot)

1. The spinal reflexes run along the inner edge of each foot from the base of the big toe to the inner-ankle. To thoroughly relax the spine, support the right foot in the palm of your left hand and stroke down the inside of the foot working from the big toe down to the heel.

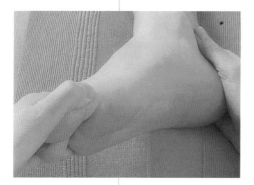

2. Support the foot under the heel with your holding hand and caterpillar-walk down the medial aspect (inside) of the foot beginning at the base of the toenail

3. This represents the top of the spine (cervical area) and, as you walk down the foot, you are covering the middle of the back (thoracic area) and the low back (lumbar area).

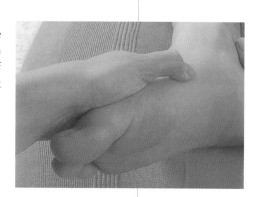

4. Now change hands, placing your holding hand at the top of the foot with your thumb on the back of the toes and your fingers wrapped around the front of the toes. Repeat the thumb-walking, working in the opposite direction from the base of the heel up to the base of the toenail.

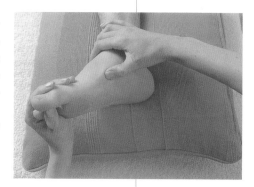

Step 9 Eyes and Ears (Base of the Toes)

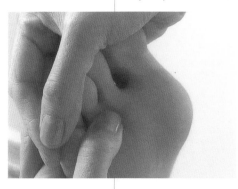

1. You are going to thumb-walk along the ridge at the base of the toes – the shoulder girdle line. Pull the toes gently back with your holding hand to make the area easy to reach – thumb on the bottom, fingers at the top. Thumb-walk across the ridge moving in both directions.

2. To locate the right eye more precisely, caterpillar-walk across the ridge and stop between the second and third toes. Use your thumb and use the hook-in and back-up technique to press firmly into the eye point.

3. Continue to caterpillar-walk and stop between the fourth and fifth toes. Press firmly into this area to treat the right ear.

Shoulder Girdle Line to Diaphragm Line

Step 1 Thyroid/Parathyroid/Thymus

The thyroid and parathyroid reflex points are located on the ball beneath the big toe. Support the toes of the right foot with the left hand. Place your right thumb just below the ball of the foot on the inside and thumb-walk from the diaphragm line in a curved direction up to between the big toe and the second toe. Return to the diaphragm line and caterpillar-walk up the foot several times until you have completely covered the area under the big toe. The thyroid is located in the centre of the pad of the ball of the foot below the big toe. As this reflex is often tender we will do pressure circles on this area.

1. Place the flat pad of your thumb onto the thyroid area and circle your thumb gently over the area several times. If there is any tenderness it should diminish after a few pressure circles.

2. The parathyroid area is found slightly to the left of the thyroid gland. Move your thumb slightly to the left and perform pressure circles on the parathyroid area.

3. The thymus is found to the right of the thyroid gland close to the spinal reflexes. Move your thumb to the right almost as far as the inside of the foot and once again use your thumb to circle over the thymus area.

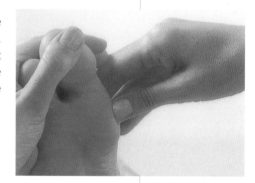

61

Step 2 Right Lung/Chest (Ball of the Foot)

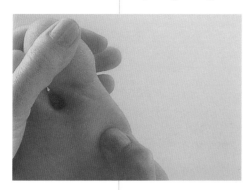

The lung area encompasses the entire ball of the foot from the shoulder girdle line to the diaphragm line. Pull the toes back slightly with the left holding hand, with the fingers cupped over the front of the toes. Start at the base of the toes and with your right thumb caterpillar-walk into vertical strips from the diaphragm line to the shoulder girdle line on the sole of the foot. Thumb-walk until the whole of the area between the shoulder girdle line and the diaphragm line has been covered.

Right Keep your lungs healthy with regular exercise.

Step 3 Right Breast/Lungs/Mammary Glands (Top of the Foot)

1. Pull the toes forward with your left hand, thumb under the sole of the foot, fingers cupped over the top of the toes. Finger-walk down the troughs on the top of the foot from the base of the toes to the diaphragm line. Cover the entire area in vertical strips. As the top of the foot is more sensitive use your index finger to do the walking. You may also use several fingers at once.

2. Alternatively you can support the foot by making a fist with your left hand and placing it under the toes. Finger-walk in the same way as before.

Diaphragm Line to the Waistline

Step 1 Liver/Gallbladder (Right Foot Only)

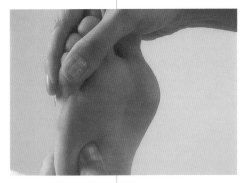

1. The liver is the largest reflex area in the foot and therefore has a large reflex area. Imagine a triangle extending up across the diaphragm line from the left-hand side of the diaphragm line to the left-hand side of the waistline and then across to the right-hand side of the diaphragm line. Bend the toes away from you to open up the reflex area and caterpillar-walk this whole area in diagonal strips in both directions.

2. Locate the gallbladder reflex which lies in between the diaphragm line and the waistline in line with the fourth toe. The gallbladder reflex appears to vary somewhat in its location, but it can feel like an indentation or a small swelling. As this is often a tender point we will use the rotation technique. Support the foot with your right hand and place the pad of your left thumb onto the gallbladder reflex. With your right holding hand, flex the foot slowly into your left thumb and rotate the foot in a circular motion around the thumb.

Step 2 Stomach/Pancreas/Duodenum

The stomach, pancreas and duodenum may be treated by working on the sole of the right foot as well as the left foot. Use your left hand to hold the foot and thumb-walk just below the diaphragm line from the inside of the foot (zone one) to approximately the centre of the foot (zone three).

Repeat the caterpillar-walking in horizontal rows until you reach the waistline. You may reverse the hands to work in the opposite direction if you wish.

Left A healthy diet will aid your digestive system.

65

Step 3 Adrenal Gland

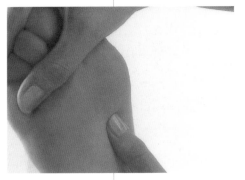

The adrenal gland is usually easily pin-pointed as it is often tender. If you pull back the toes a thick tendon running from the big toe to the heel will protrude. The adrenal reflex point is located midway between the diaphragm and the waistline on the medial side (inside) of this tendon. With your right hand holding the right foot, fingers wrapped around the top of the foot, place your left thumb on the adrenal point. Use your right hand to flex the foot onto your left thumb and rotate the foot around the thumb.

Right Your adrenal glands help you to deal with stressful situations such as examinations by releasing hormones.

Below The Waistline

Step 1 Right Kidney/Ureter Tube/Bladder

1. Part of the kidney is located just above the waistline between zones two and three. However the other half of the kidney, ureter tube and bladder are located below the waistline. After you have gently rotated the adrenal reflex move the thumb down slightly and you will have found the kidney reflex point. With the tip of your thumb pointing toward the toes, press into the area and circle your thumb gently over the kidney area several times.

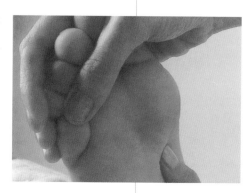

2. Turn the thumb around so that it is facing downward, then caterpillar-walk down the ureter reflex toward the inside of the foot where the bladder reflex is situated beneath the inner ankle bone.

The bladder area can often look slightly puffy. You may either thumb-walk or rotate on the bladder reflex.

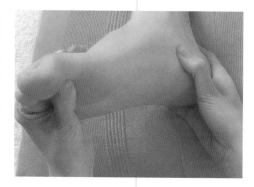

Step 2 Small Intestines

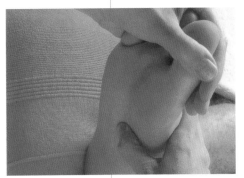

Hold the right foot back with your left hand and caterpillar-walk in horizontal rows from just below the waistline to the pelvic floor line from the medial aspect (inside) of the foot as far as zone four. You may work the whole of this area with your right thumb.

Right Make the most of your leisure time to relieve stress that can cause stomach/ intestinal discomfort. Relaxing after a meal will aid digestion.

Step 3 Ileocecal Valve/Ascending and Transverse Colon

1. The colon wraps around the small intestine. To locate the ileocecal valve run your finger along zone five down the lower third of the sole of the foot toward the heel. Just above the pelvic floor line the hollow spot that you may feel is the ileocecal valve reflex point. Using your left thumb press onto the point and circle several times over the reflex area.

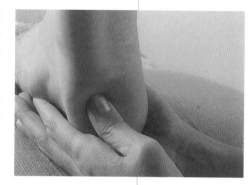

2. Then caterpillar-walk with your left thumb up the ascending colon in zone five toward the waistline. You may feel a swelling either on or just below the waistline. This is the hepatic flexure. Circle over this area several times.

3. Then turn the thumb 90 degrees to the right and caterpillar-walk horizontally along the transverse colon reflex following the waistline until you reach the inside of the sole of the foot.

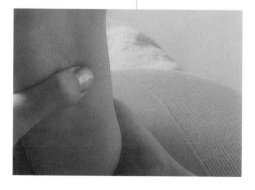

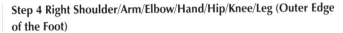

Step 4 Right Shoulder/Arm/Elbow/Hand/Hip/Knee/Leg (Outer Edge of the Foot)

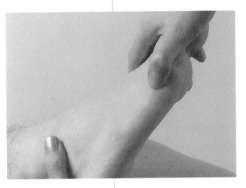

1. The areas corresponding to the joints of the body are situated along the outer edge of the foot. (Remember the spine runs the length of the inside of the foot.)

Hold the toes of the right foot with your right hand and with your left thumb caterpillar-walk vertically up the outer edge of the foot from the heel area up to the little toe.

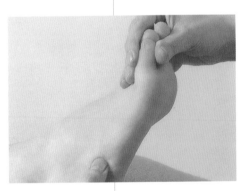

2. If you wish you may cup the right heel with your left hand and repeat the thumb-walking in the opposite direction from the little toe to the heel. If you come across any areas that are tender then gently circle your thumb over them several times. The shoulder reflex on the bony prominence at the base of the little toe is likely to need attention.

Alternatively you may use your index finger to cover this area.

Step 5 Sciatic Nerve Line/Pelvic Area

The area around the Achilles tendon is not only worked for problems with the sciatic nerve, but also for chronic ailments related to the prostate, uterus and the rectum.

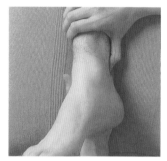

1. Hold the right foot with your left hand and place your right thumb approximately 15 cm (6 in) above the inner ankle bone. Thumb-walk down the Achilles tendon area toward the heel.

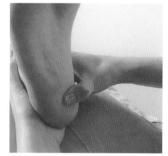

2. Continue to thumb-walk across the sciatic nerve line on the hard heel pad of the right foot.

3. Finger-walk or thumb-walk up the outside of the foot along the Achilles tendon, changing hands if necessary.

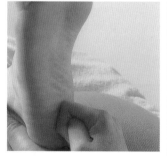

4. When there are problems with the pelvis it is very effective to work across the heel pad. Cup the foot with your left hand and gently work the area with your knuckles in a circular direction.

Step 6 Prostate/Uterus (Below Inside of Ankle)

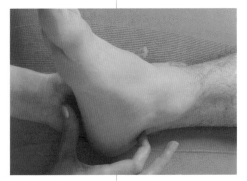

All the reproductive organ reflexes are situated around the ankle area. To locate the prostate/uterus point place the index finger on the inner ankle bone and the third finger on the tip of the heel. Imagine a straight line running between your two fingers. The prostate/uterus lies in the middle of this imaginary line. Place the index finger onto the point and perform small circular pressure circles on the area.

Right Reflexology can aid prostate health and well-being.

Step 7 Vas Deferens/Lymph/Groin/Fallopian Tube (Across the Top of the Foot)

1. Thumb-walk or finger-walk from the inside of the ankle across the top of the foot to the outside of the ankle. This area should be walked in both directions.

2. This area can be quite sensitive. Remember if you find a tender area, gently massage it in a circular direction.

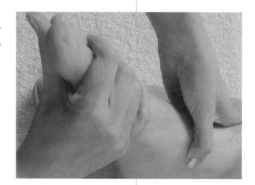

Step 8 Right Testicle/Ovary (Below Outside of the Ankle)

1. Locate the testicle/ovary reflex by drawing an imaginary diagonal line from the outer ankle bone to the top of the heel and finding the mid-point.

2. Now you should perform small circular movements over this area with your index finger.

Step 9 Completing the Right Foot

Using both hands, stroke the whole foot working up from the toes, gliding around the ankle bones and back again. These stroking movements should ensure that any toxins which have been released during the reflexology sequence are dispersed and the right foot is completely relaxed. Now cover up the right foot.

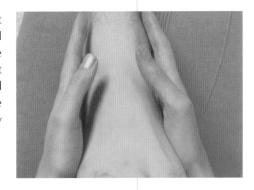

Left Reflexology helps to keep your body and all it's systems in the best possible shape.

Reflexology Sequence Left Foot

Now try a complete sequence on the left foot. These pages give you a quick reminder of the techniques being used. In the following sequence (pp. 77-103) are all steps you will need,

Relaxation Techniques

These techniques have already been described in detail in the previous chapter (see pp33–41). Here only the basic movement for each technique is shown.

Effleurage/stroking p.33

Metatarsal kneading p.34

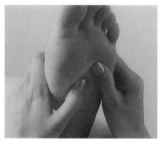

Alternate thumb rotations p.35

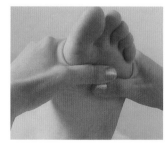

Spreading the foot p.36

Spinal stroking p.37

Spinal twist p.38

Toe loosening p.39

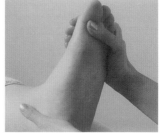

Ankle rotations p.40

Foot rocking p.41

Tension Release

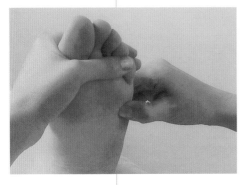

Diaphragm/Solar Plexus

1. To locate the solar plexus and diaphragm, gently pull the toes backwards with your left hand. Hold the toes with your thumb on the sole of the foot, fingers on the top.

2. Walk across the diaphragm line with your right thumb, working from the outside of the foot toward the inside.

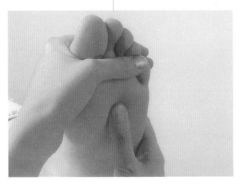

3. When you reach the solar plexus press gently into it as the receiver breathes in and release the pressure as they breathe out. Repeat several times.

Head and Neck Area

Step 1 Head and Brain Area (Back and Sides of the Big Toe)

1. Wrap the fingers of your right hand over the front of the toes with your thumb under the back of the toes. Using your left thumb, thumb-walk from the outer edge of the base of the big toe.

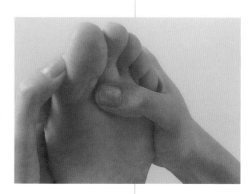

2. Now continue walking up the outside of the toe, over the top and finally down the inside.

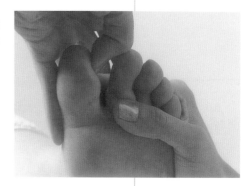

3. With your left thumb-walk up the back of the big toe from the base to the tip several times to cover the whole area.

Step 2 Pituitary Gland (Big Toe)

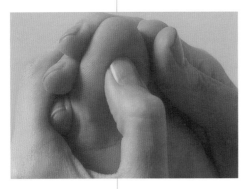

To locate the pituitary gland find the widest point of the big toe and draw an imaginary line. The pituitary gland lies approximately in the centre of this line, but remember that you often have to search for it. Place the fingers of your right hand over the front of the toes and your thumb under the back of the toes. Using the hook-in and back-up technique, press the pituitary gland with the corner of your left thumb.

Step 3 Face (Front of the Big Toe)

Wrap your left hand around the top of the foot just below the base of the toes, left thumb under the sole of the foot, fingers on the top. Use your right index finger to walk down the front of the big toe, from the tip to the base until the whole of the area has been covered. You may also use your index and middle finger if you are highly coordinated.

Step 4 Neck (Base of the Big Toe)

1. Support the left foot with your left hand and grasp the big toe between your right thumb and index finger. Rotate the big toe clockwise and anticlockwise to improve the mobility of the neck

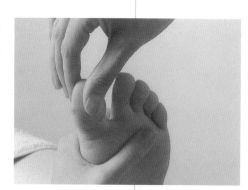

2. Now wrap your right hand around the top of the foot, fingers on the top, thumb on the sole. Walk across the back of the base of the big toe using your left thumb.

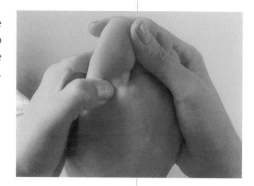

3. Use your index finger to walk across the base of the front of the toe, working from outside to inside.

Step 5 Sinuses (Back, Sides and Top of the Small Toes)

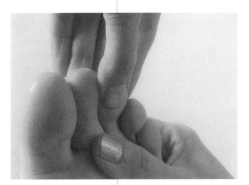

1. Support the left foot between the thumb and fingers of your right hand, thumb on the sole of the foot, fingers over the front of the toes. With your left thumb use very small caterpillar steps to walk from the top to the base of each toe.

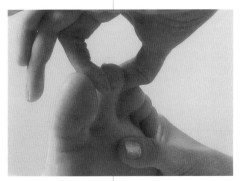

2. Use your left thumb, index finger, or thumb and index finger together, to walk down the sides of each toe. If you prefer you may walk up the toes instead of down, but it is often more effective to work down the toes. It also makes more sense as you are draining toward the lymph glands.

Step 6 Teeth (Front of the Toes)

Wrap your right hand around the top of the foot. Commencing at the base finger-walk with your left index finger down the fronts of the small toes.

Step 7 Upper Lymphatics (Between the Toes)

Support the foot with your left hand. Use the thumb and index finger of your right hand to gently squeeze the webbing between each of the toes.

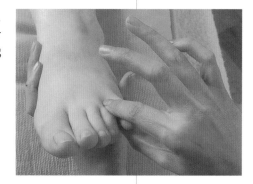

Step 8 Spine (Inner Edge of the Foot)

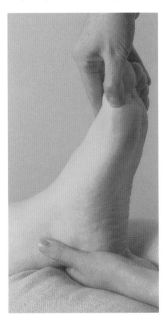 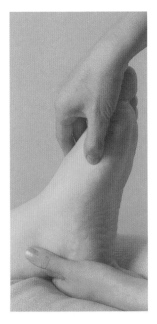

1. Cup the heel of the left foot with your left hand. Using your right thumb, caterpillar-walk down the inside of the foot from the base of the big toenail to the heel.

2. If you feel any gritty or tender areas gently massage the crystals away.

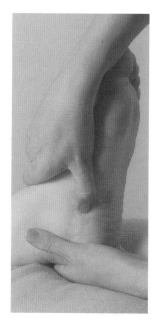

Below You can perform some reflexology treatments on your own feet. See page 136.

3. You may also walk in the opposite direction, from the heel to the base of the toenail.

85

Step 9 Eyes And Ears (Base of the Toes)

1. Pull the toes gently back with your holding hand and thumb-walk across the ridge at the base of the toes in both directions.

Right Making time to relax and recharge your batteries will benefit your body and your mind.

2. To locate the left eye point, walk across the base of the toes and stop between the second and third toes. Press firmly into this point using the hook-in and back-up technique.

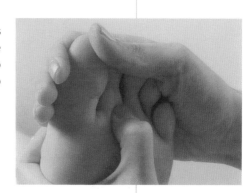

3. To find the left ear point, continue your caterpillar-walk as far as between the fourth and fifth toes. Use the hook-in and back-up technique on this area.

87

Shoulder Girdle Line to Diaphragm Line

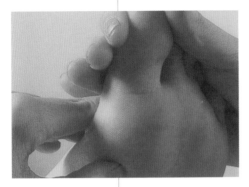

Step 1 Thyroid/Parathyroid/Thymus

1. Support the toes with your right hand. Place your left thumb below the ball on the diaphragm line just on the inside of the foot.

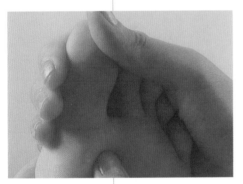

2. Walk in a curved direction up to between the big and the second toe. Caterpillar-walk the pad under the big toe until you have completely covered the area.

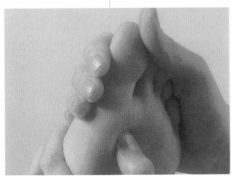

3. Find the thyroid point in the centre of the pad of the ball of the foot below the big toe. Place your left thumb onto the thyroid reflex and circle gently over the area several times.

4. Move your left thumb over to the right to contact the parathyroid area and perform pressure circles on this area.

5. Slide your left thumb over toward the inside of the foot and rotate it gently over the thymus point.

Step 2 Left Lung/Chest (Ball of the Foot)

1. To treat the left lung, work across the entire area from the shoulder girdle line to the diaphragm line.

2. Pull the toes back with your right-hand, fingers wrapped around the front of the foot, thumb underneath.

3. With your left thumb, thumb-walk in vertical strips from the diaphragm line to the shoulder girdle line.

4. To thoroughly de-congest the area, use your left thumb to walk across the area in horizontal strips.

Step 3 Left Lung/Breast/Mammary Glands (Top of the Foot)

1. Pull all the toes very GENTLY back toward you with your left hand, fingers on top of the foot, thumb underneath. Use your right index finger or your index and middle finger to walk down the front of the foot in vertical strips as far as the diaphragm line.

2. Alternatively, make a fist with one of your hands and place it under the toes as a support. Now finger-walk the lung/breast area in the same way as shown in previous step.

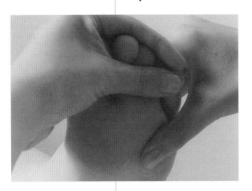

Step 4 Heart Area

1. Hold the foot in your left hand and wrap your right hand over the foot, thumb on the sole, fingers on the top. With your right thumb gently massage the upper third of the sole of the foot from the shoulder girdle line to the diaphragm line, working in a circular direction.

2. Now repeat these movements using your right index finger on the top of the foot. As you work the heart area you will also be working the left lung as these two reflexes overlap considerably.

Warning

The heart is located mostly on the left foot between the shoulder girdle line and the diaphragm line. If any pain or sensitivity is felt in this area then do NOT increase your pressure. Deep pressure should NEVER be used on this area immediately after a heart attack or if a pacemaker has been fitted.

Diaphragm Line to Waistline

Step 1 Stomach/Pancreas/Duodenum

Hold the foot in the right hand, thumb on the sole, fingers on the top. Place your thumb just below the inside edge of the diaphragm line. Thumb-walk in horizontal rows from zone one to zone four until the entire area from diaphragm line to waistline has been covered.

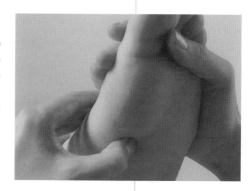

Step 2 Spleen

To treat the spleen, which is ONLY found on the left foot, hold the foot with your left hand. Place your right thumb just below the outside edge of the diaphragm line and caterpillar-walk from zone five to zone four in horizontal rows.

93

Step 3 Left Adrenal Gland

1. To locate the adrenal gland, pull back the toes until a thick tendon running from the big toe to the heel protrudes. The reflex point is found midway between the diaphragm and waistlines on the inside of this tendon. Hold the left foot with your left hand, placing your right thumb onto the adrenal point.

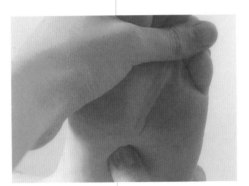

2. Use your left hand to flex the foot onto your right thumb and rotate the foot around it.

Below the Waistline

Step 1 Left Kidney/Ureter/Bladder

1. After you have gently treated the left adrenal gland, move your right thumb down slightly. With the pad of your right thumb pointing toward the toes, press into the area and circle it gently over the kidney area several times.

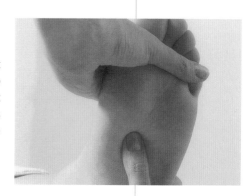

2. Now turn your thumb around so that it is facing downward and caterpillar-walk down the ureter reflex toward the inside of the foot – the bladder reflex is found beneath the inner ankle bone.

3. Either thumb-walk over this point or rotate on the bladder reflex.

Step 2 Small Intestines

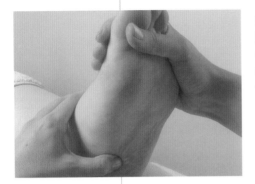

Hold the left foot back with your right hand and with your left thumb, thumb-walk in horizontal rows from the inside the foot as far as zone four from just below the waistline to the pelvic floor line.

Right A healthy diet will help to keep your digestive system working well.

Step 3 Transverse Colon/Descending Colon/Sigmoid Colon

1. Hold the toes of the left foot in your right hand. Place your left thumb just below the waistline on the inner side of the sole of the foot.

2. Caterpillar-walk across the transverse colon, following the waistline until you reach zone five on the outer edge of the left foot.

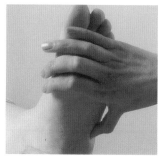 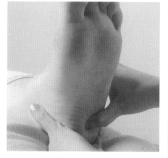

3. Change hands and, using the right thumb, thumb-walk down zone five which is the descending colon toward the heel.

4. Just before you reach the pelvic floor line turn the right thumb 45 degrees diagonally to the left until you reach the sciatic line. Swivel the right thumb around and circle several times to treat the sigmoid colon. Then continue caterpillar-walking toward the bladder area.

97

Step 4 Left Shoulder/Arm/Elbow/Hand/Hip/Knee/Leg (Outer Edge of the Foot)

1. Hold the toes of the left foot with your left hand and with your right thumb caterpillar-walk along the outer edge of the foot.

2. Continue caterpillar-walking until you have covered the whole area – from the heel to the little toe.

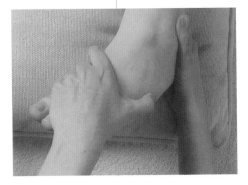

3. Now cup the left heel with your right hand and walk your left thumb in the opposite direction – from the little toe to the heel.

Step 5 Sciatic Nerve Line/Pelvic Area

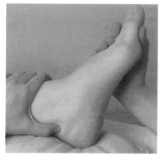

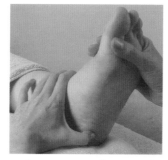

1. Hold the ball of the left foot with your right hand and place your left thumb 15 cm (6 in) above the inner heel. Thumb-walk down the Achilles tendon toward the heel.

2. Continue to walk across the hard heel pad all along the sciatic nerve line.

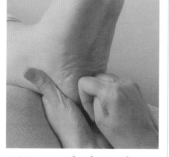

3. With your right thumb, thumb-walk up the outside of the foot behind the ankle bone along the Achilles tendon.

4. Now cup the foot with your left hand and work across the pad with your knuckles in a circular direction.

Step 6 Uterus/Prostate (Below Inside of Ankle)

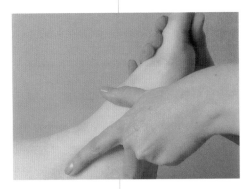

1. To pinpoint this reflex area, place the index finger on the inner ankle bone and the third finger on the tip of the heel. Imagine a straight line running between your two fingers.

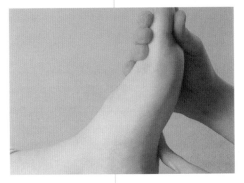

2. In the middle of this imaginary line is the uterus/prostate point. Place your index finger on this point and perform small circular pressure circles on this area.

Step 7 Fallopian Tube/Vas Deferens/Lymph/Groin
(Across the Top of the Foot)

1. Using your left thumb-walk from the inside of the ankle across the top of the foot to the outside of the ankle.

2. Now continue walking in the same direction.

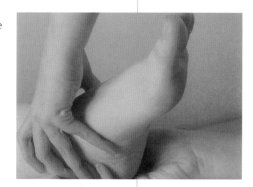

Step 8 Left Ovary/Testicle (Below Outside of the Ankle)

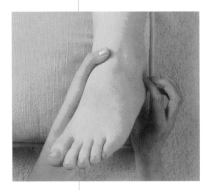

Draw an imaginary diagonal line from the outer ankle bone to the tip of the heel and find the mid-point. Perform small circular movements all over this area using your right index finger.

Completing the Left Foot

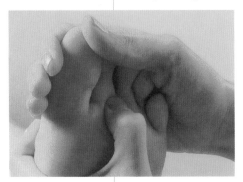

To completely disperse any toxins which have been released during the treatment, stroke the left foot from the toes up to the ankle bones and back again as many times as you like.

Well done. You have now completed both of the feet.

The Finale

1. Uncover both feet and return to any reflex points that were tender during the reflexology session in order to give them further attention.

2. Use any of your favourite relaxation techniques.

3. Very gently and lightly run your fingertips down the tops and sides of the feet, barely touching the skin.

4. To complete your reflexology session carry out the solar plexus release. Place both thumbs into the hollows on the soles of the feet at the diaphragm line. Press gently and slowly into the solar plexus reflex points as the receiver breathes in. Gradually release your pressure as he/she breathes out.

5. Cover the feet and leave the receiver to relax for while.

6. When they get up give them a large glass of water to drink and encourage them to drink plenty of water over the next 24 hours to flush out the toxins.

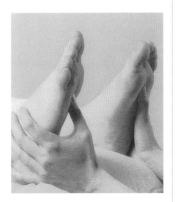

Reflexology for Common Ailments

The beauty of reflexology is that it is a simple, straightforward healing technique that you can use to treat a wide variety of common ailments. Be prepared to try out different approaches and be aware of painful areas and tender spots. Let the receiver be your guide and be ready to adapt your approach accordingly.

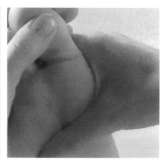

Diaphragm line position

Solar Plexus: Apply pressure to encourage a state of relaxation.

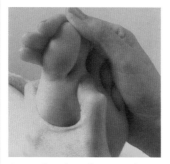

Eyes: Thumb-walk across the ridge at base of the toes. Press into eye point between toes two and three.

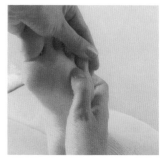

Ears: Thumb-walk across ridge at the base of the toes. Press into the ear point between toes four and five.

Treatments

During a reflexology session, tender areas may indicate certain imbalances. After a treatment you can return to these sensitive spots to give them more attention. Once you are familiar with the Basic Reflexology Treatments (pp24-31) use these techniques to treat specific areas.

This section looks at some common ailments and suggests areas to concentrate on. Many of these areas feature in all or most of the recommended treatments and are illustrated here. Other specific areas are illustrated throughout the section. If you are uncertain of any point, please refer back to these pages.

Face: Finger-walk the front of the big toe.

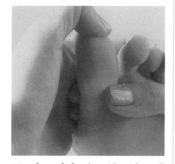

Head and brain: Thumb-walk the back and sides of the big toe.

Heart area: Thumb circles on the upper third of the sole of the foot and make index finger circles on top of foot.

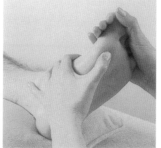

Lung/chest area: Thumb-walk the chest area on the sole of the foot from the diaphragm line to the shoulder girdle line.

105

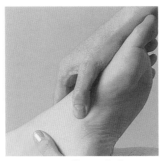

Spine: Caterpillar-walk down the inside of the foot. Repeat walking up the foot.

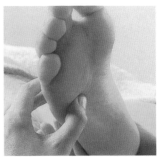

Liver: Thumb-walk the triangular liver area between the diaphragm line and the waistline.

Kidneys: Circle over the kidney area.

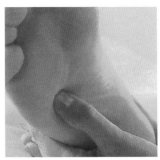

Gallbladder: Rotate onto the gallbladder area.

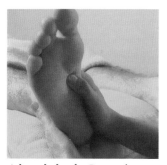

Adrenal glands: Rotate the adrenal gland.

Upper lymphatics: Gently squeeze the webbing between each of the toes.

Pituitary gland: Hook-in and back-up on the centre of the big toe.

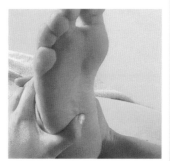

Transverse colon: Thumb-walk across the transverse colon.

Circulatory Problems

Heart disease is one of the main causes of premature death in the developed world. Contributory factors include poor diet, obesity, high stress levels, lack of exercise, genetic predisposition and smoking. Reflexology is excellent for improving the circulation, balancing the blood pressure and reducing stress on the heart. These treatments are explored in more detail on the following pages.

Below Exercise, such as Tai Chi, will help to reduce the symptoms of angina.

Angina

Angina is caused by a lack of oxygen reaching the heart muscle, usually as a result of a hardening of the arteries. Chest pain is experienced due to the decreased blood and oxygen supply to the heart tissue. Most patients with angina complain of chest discomfort rather than actual pain, describing a pressure, heaviness, tightness, squeezing, burning or choking sensation.

Causes of Angina Anything that causes the coronary arteries to narrow can be linked with angina, including:

- High-fat diet
- Stress
- Lack of exercise
- Hereditary factors
- Smoking

Lifestyle Adjustments (to reduce the effects of angina) Dietary and lifestyle changes can improve blood pressure control and decrease the risk of associated health complications:

- Eat a healthy diet – avoid junk food, sugar, salt, fried foods and saturated animal fats. Instead eat plenty of fresh fruit and vegetables, fibre and virgin olive oil
- Give up smoking
- Take regular, gentle physical exercise, for example a 20-minute walk daily, or a Tai Chi or yoga class

Reflexology Treatment
- Heart area
- Liver – to help normalise cholesterol
- Adrenals – to relieve stress
- Solar plexus
- Diaphragm – to deepen breathing
- Lungs and chest – to relax and open up chest area

Heart area (left foot): Thumb circles on upper third of the sole, index finger circles on the top of foot:
- Place the flat pad of the thumb onto the upper third of the sole, press slowly into the area and circle the thumb.
- Circle index finger on top of the foot.
- Deep pressure should NEVER be used on this area after a heart attack or if a pacemaker has been fitted.

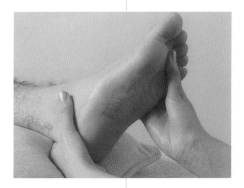

Solar Plexus (right foot): Applying pressure to this area encourages a state of relaxation:
- Place your thumbs onto the solar plexus reflex on each foot.
- Press very gently and slowly several times.

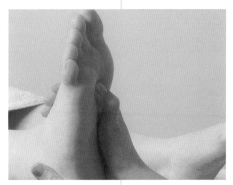

Hypertension (High Blood Pressure)

High blood pressure is a fairly common disorder, which increases with age. It is a chronic medical condition in which the blood pressure in the arteries is elevated, requiring the heart to work harder than normal to circulate blood through the blood vessels and around the body. Hypertension is a major risk factor for stroke, heart attacks, heart failure, arterial disease and kidney disease. Even moderate elevation of arterial blood pressure is associated with a shortened life expectancy.

Above Eating plenty of fresh fruit and vegetables will help to keep high blood pressure in check.

Causes of Hypertension Though the exact causes of hypertension are usually unknown, there are several factors that have been strongly associated with the condition. These include:

• Stress
• Obesity (or being overweight)
• Diabetes
• Smoking
• Family history (genetic predisposition)
• High levels of alcohol consumption
• Kidney disease
• Adrenal and thyroid problems

Lifestyle Adjustments (to reduce blood pressure) Dietary and lifestyle changes can improve blood pressure control and decrease the risk of associated health complications:

• Avoid salt, sugar and saturated fats
• Eat lots of fruit, vegetables, fibre (especially oats, which are proven to reduce cholesterol) and garlic
• Give up smoking and reduce alcohol and caffeine intake
• Reduce stress
• Take gentle, regular exercise, for example, a 20-minute walk daily, or a Tai Chi or yoga class

Reflexology Treatment
- Heart area
- Kidneys
- Adrenal glands – to reduce stress
- Solar plexus
- Diaphragm – to deepen breathing
- Lungs and chest – to relax the chest area

Kidneys (left foot): Thumb-circle over the kidney point:
- Press slowly into the area and circle the thumb.

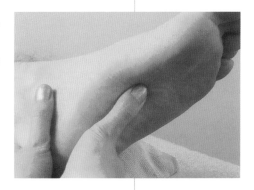

Working from the kidney towards the bladder (left foot):
- Circle over kidney point, turn thumb and caterpillar-walk down the ureter reflex toward the inside of the foot, where the bladder reflex is situated beneath the inner ankle bone.
- The bladder area can often look slightly puffy. You may either thumb-walk or rotate on the bladder reflex.

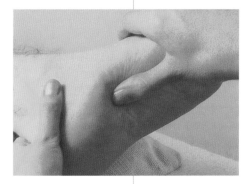

Digestive Problems

Most people suffer at some time or other from a digestive disorder. The digestive system is very prone to upset, particularly through stress. Imbalance can be caused by emotions such as anger, tension and fear, or by eating too quickly. Many of us snack on junk foods and refined foods that contain little nutritional value and which also may contain harmful colourings and preservatives. We also drink far too much coffee and soft carbonated drinks with caffeine in them. Our bodies would prefer six to eight glasses of water a day!

Reflexology is an excellent tool for releasing tension and assisting the process of digestion and elimination. A doctor should, of course, always be consulted about any digestive problem if it is persistent or is accompanied by weight loss, blood in the faeces or a general sense of being unwell.

Below Taking time to enjoy your food will help to reduce incidences of heartburn and indigestion.

Indigestion/Heartburn (dyspepsia)

Indigestion is a term that people use to describe a range of different symptoms relating to the stomach and gastrointestinal system. The most common symptom is pain, usually after eating, in the upper part of the abdomen underneath the rib cage. This might be mild or severe, stabbing or a generalised soreness.

Causes of Indigestion Indigestion is very common. It can be caused by:
- Excessive eating and drinking, rushing or not chewing food properly
- Eating refined foods such as cakes and biscuits, fatty foods, hot and spicy or rich foods
- Stress, which increases stomach acid
- Smoking

Lifestyle Adjustments (to reduce indigestion or heartburn)

Dietary and lifestyle changes can regulate the gastrointestinal tract and reduce the likelihood of indigestion or heartburn occurring.

- Avoid stressful situations
- Reduce foods that cause heartburn (as listed opposite)
- Regular exercise also helps to keep the gastrointestinal tract working efficiently and reduces the risk of indigestion

Reflexology Treatment
- Stomach/pancreas/duodenum
- Liver/gallbladder – if there is nausea
- Solar plexus – to reduce tension
- Adrenal gland – to reduce inflammation

Stomach/pancreas/duodenum (right foot): Thumb-walk from the inside of the foot to approximately the centre of the foot:

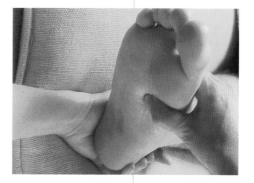

- Thumb-walk just below the diaphragm line from the inside of the foot (zone one) to approximately the centre of the foot (zone three).
- Repeat the caterpillar-walking in horizontal rows until you reach the waistline.

Liver/gallbladder (right foot): Thumb-walk triangular liver area between diaphragm line and waistline. Rotate onto gallbladder:

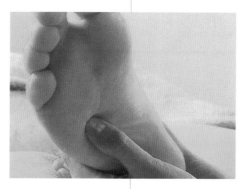

- Bend toes away from you to open up the reflex area, caterpillar-walk whole area in diagonal strips in both directions.
- Place the pad of your left thumb onto the gallbladder reflex. With your right holding hand, flex the foot slowly into your left thumb and rotate the foot in a circular motion.

Above Drink plenty of water to help to keep your bowel healthy.

Constipation

Constipation is a common condition that affects people of all ages. It can mean that you are not passing stools regularly or are unable to completely empty your bowels.

Causes It's often difficult to identify the cause. However, there are a number of things that increase the risk of constipation, including:

- Poor diet and inadequate intake of water
- Lack of exercise
- Stress and tension
- Certain drugs such as too many laxatives, which make the bowel lazy, antibiotics, painkillers, steroids and diuretics

Irritable Bowel Syndrome (IBS)

This disorder is becoming increasingly prevalent and is characterised by pain in the abdominal area, which can be very intense and a combination of constipation and diarrhoea.

Causes The exact cause of IBS is unknown, but most experts agree that it's related to disruption of the normal digestion process. This may be caused by a change in your body's ability to move food through your digestive system, or it may be due to you becoming more sensitive to pain from your gut.

- Stress is a major trigger of irritable bowel syndrome
- The factors that can cause an attack vary enormously but common culprits include dairy foods, wheat, chocolate, coffee and alcohol

Lifestyle Adjustments (to ease the symptoms of constipation and IBS)

There is no cure for IBS, but the symptoms can be managed by making changes to your diet and lifestyle:

- Avoid stress
- Eat a healthy high-fibre diet to increase the frequency and quantity of bowel movements

- Drink six to eight glasses of water per day
- Do not ignore the urge to move your bowels
- Avoid prolonged use of laxatives, which can make the bowel lazy

Reflexology Treatment for Constipation and IBS
- Small intestines
- Ileocecal valve, which controls movement between the small and large intestines
- Large intestines:
  – ascending colon
  – transverse (right foot) colon
- Chronic rectum
- Solar plexus – to reduce tension

For IBS only:
- Adrenals – to reduce inflammation and irritation within the digestive tract

See sequence below:
- Hook-in and back-up on ileocecal reflex
- Thumb-walk up ascending colon
- Rotate on hepatic flexure
- Thumb-walk across transverse colon
- Rotate on solar plexus
- Rotate on adrenals

Ascending colon (right foot)

Ileocecal valve (right foot)

115

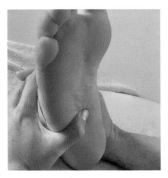

Transverse colon

Solar Plexus

Adrenals

Liver/Gallbladder Problems

The gallbladder should always be treated with care. Never massage it vigorously if there are gallstones. Gentle reflexology on this area, however, is often very successful: certain patients awaiting operations have had their gallstones eliminated with the help of reflexology.

Gallstones

Gallstones are formed from cholesterol, bile pigments and calcium compounds. They can cause colicky pain when found in the gallbladder and are common but cause no symptoms in two out of three people who have them. If they are found in the bile ducts (which connect the gallbladder and liver to the duodenum) then the pain can be excruciating. Gallstones can lead to inflammation of the gallbladder, jaundice and pancreatitis.

Causes It is thought that gallstones develop because of an imbalance in the chemical make-up of the bile inside the gallbladder. In most cases the levels of cholesterol in the bile become too high and the excess cholesterol forms into stones.

You are more at risk of developing gallstones if you:

- Eat a fatty diet
- Are obese (or overweight)

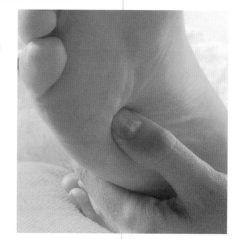

Lifestyle Adjustments (to reduce the likelihood of developing gallstones) There is no guaranteed way to prevent gallstones, but you can lower your risk:

- Eat a low-fat, low-sugar diet that is high in fibre.
- Drink fresh lemon squeezed into warm water.

Liver

Reflexology Treatment

- Liver
- Gallbladder

117

Genito-Urinary Problems

Women in particular can suffer from a whole host of conditions as the hormones are so easily unbalanced. Problems with the kidneys, urinary and reproductive systems can cause discomfort, inconvenience and embarrassment, as well as having more serious consequences. Reflexology is excellent for relieving both the physical and emotional symptoms that can occur. However, always consult a doctor if your symptoms continue to reoccur since untreated bladder infections can cause kidney infections.

Cystitis

Cystitis is an inflammation of the inner lining of the bladder, giving rise to frequent urination, burning or stinging sensations, low backache and feeling run down. Cystitis usually passes within a few days, or sometimes may need treatment with antibiotics.

Causes Cystitis is usually caused by an infection or irritation:
- Infection passing from the urethral opening into the bladder. The bacteria can come from the vagina or the intestines via the anus.
- Stress can often precede an attack of cystitis.

Above Drinking cranberry juice is said to help to prevent cystitis.

Lifestyle Adjustments (to reduce the likelihood of developing cystitis) It's not always possible to prevent cystitis, but you can take some steps to help avoid the condition:
- Some people find that certain types of food and drink make their cystitis worse: for example, coffee, fruit juice or spicy foods. If you know there are foods that trigger your cystitis it's best to avoid them
- Don't wait to go if you need to urinate and always empty your bladder fully
- Drink cranberry juice
- Increase fluid intake to flush out the bladder
- Avoid using perfumed bubble bath, soap and talcum powder

Reflexology Treatment
- Kidneys
- Bladder – the bladder area will often look raised and puffy where there is an infection
- Lower spine – for pain relief
- Adrenals – for inflammation

Always work FROM the kidney towards the bladder. NEVER go back up – otherwise you could transfer the infection. A kidney infection is much more serious than a bladder infection.

Adrenals (left foot): Rotate adrenal gland:
- Hold the left foot in the left hand. Place your right thumb on the adrenal point, located midway between the diaphragm and the waistline.
- Use your left hand to flex the foot and rotate the foot around the thumb.

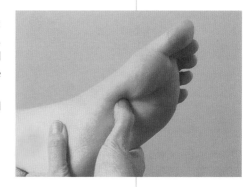

Bladder (left foot): Thumb-walk and rotate on the bladder reflex. The bladder area can often look slightly puffy.

Above Eating calcium-rich foods can help to reduce the symptoms of menstrual problems.

Menstrual Problems

These include premenstrual syndrome (PMS), painful periods, absent or scanty periods and menopause. Reflexology can relax the body and mind, give pain relief from menstrual cramps and aid the elimination of excess fluid from the body.

Causes Many women experience physical and mood changes around the time of their period, but for some it can be a particularly difficult time. It's not known what causes PMS, but the normal hormonal changes that occur during the menstrual cycle are thought to be involved and PMS can be to be linked to:
• Hormonal imbalances
• Stress

Lifestyle Adjustments (to reduce the symptoms of menstrual problems) Reducing stress levels and making changes in diet and exercise may help to relieve symptoms
• Reduce salt, which leads to fluid retention
• Reduce sugar and caffeine, which aggravate mood swings
• Increase fibre intake
• Take a vitamin B-complex supplement
• Gentle exercise such as yoga and Tai Chi
• If you are menopausal increase calcium-rich foods – e.g. fish especially sardines, sunflower, pumpkin, sesame seeds and nuts

Reflexology Treatment (see opposite page)
• All reproductive areas: ovaries, uterus, fallopian tubes
• Kidneys – to remove excess fluid
• Breasts – to alleviate soreness
• Pituitary gland – to balance hormones
• Solar plexus – to relax
• Spine – to relieve back strain and cramps

Ovaries (left foot): Carry out pressure circles with index finger reflex located midway between outer ankle bone and tip of heel:

- Perform small circular movements over this area with your index finger.

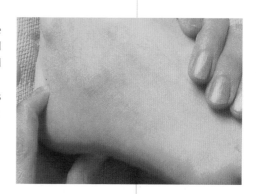

Fallopian tubes (left foot): Thumb-walk inside of the ankle. This area can be quite sensitive. Remember: if you find a tender area, gently massage it in a circular direction.

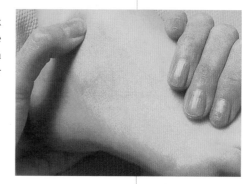

Breast area (right foot): Finger-walk the front of the foot from the base of the toes to diaphragm line:

- Use your right index finger or your index and middle finger to walk down the front of the foot in vertical strips as far as the diaphragm line.

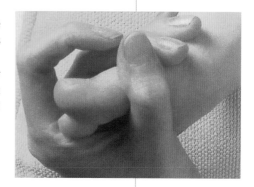

Head and Neck Problems

Your head weighs as much as a bowling ball. The vertebrae of your neck (cervical spine) support the weight of your head and all its motions. When your neck bones are not positioned properly, the result is a tightening of the muscles and irritation of the nerves that connect with your head. Common problems affecting this area include headaches, migraine and nasal problems such as catarrh, sinusitis and also hay fever.

Below Reflexology has been shown to be successful in the treatment of headaches.

Headaches/Migraine

Most of us suffer from headaches at some time – the majority of which originate in the neck and shoulders. The really unlucky ones suffer from migraine, a one-sided headache characterised by intense pain and sometimes sickness and blurred vision. Some people also have other symptoms, such as nausea and sensitivity to light.

Causes Typically, head and neck pain is brought on by stress, both emotional and physical, which can be caused by:
• Anxiety
• Tension in the neck
• Hormonal imbalances
• Irregular meals (low blood sugar and/or dehydration)
• Certain foods causing an allergic reaction
• Tiredness and overuse of the eyes
• Shock

Lifestyle Adjustments (to reduce the head and neck problems) The effectiveness of any lifestyle change in reducing your symptoms will depend on whether your neck pain is caused by activities, an injury, or another medical condition. You may see an improvement by:
• Reducing your stress levels
• If you suffer with migraine try avoiding chocolate, cheese, drinks

with caffeine in, especially coffee, alcohol, plus red wine and food additives
• Exercise can relieve tension and loosen tight muscles

Reflexology Treatment
• Head and brain area
• Spine – with emphasis on the neck area
• Pituitary gland – to balance the hormones
• Liver – to reduce toxicity and nausea (the entire digestive system may be worked to improve elimination)
• Eyes
• Solar plexus – to reduce stress and tension

Head and brain (left foot): Thumb-walk the back and sides of the big toe:
• Thumb-walk from the outer edge of the base of the big toe up the outside, over the top and down the inside.
• Thumb-walk up the back of the big toe from the base to the tip.

Spine (left foot): Caterpillar-walk down the inside of the foot. Repeat walking up the foot:
• Using your right thumb, caterpillar-walk down the inside of the foot from the base of the big toenail to the heel and back up the foot.
• If you feel any gritty or tender areas gently massage the crystals away.

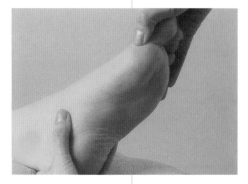

Above A steam inhalation can help to clear a blocked nose.

Nasal Problems

Your sinuses are hollow air spaces within the bones between your eyes, behind your cheekbones and in your forehead. They produce mucus, which helps keep the inside of your nose moist. That, in turn, helps protect against dust, allergens and pollutants. If the tissue in your nose is swollen it can block the sinus passages, your sinuses can't drain and you may feel pain. Reflexology is excellent for nasal problems and in particular sinusitis and hay fever. Some sufferers find that regular treatment commencing a few months prior to the hay fever season is highly effective.

Causes The treatment of nasal congestion generally depends on the underlying cause, which can be:
- Infections and the after-effects of a cold
- Environmental triggers, such as pollen or dust causing allergic responses
- Deviated septum (resulting in one smaller nostril that is prone to becoming blocked).

Lifestyle Adjustments (to prevent nasal congestion) Nasal congestion has many causes and can cause mild facial and head pain and a degree of discomfort. Significant congestion may interfere with sleep, cause snoring and affect the ears and hearing. The effectiveness of any lifestyle change will depend on the underlying cause, but trying any of the list below may help to reduce symptoms:
- Avoid dairy foods, which increase the production of mucus
- Take a steam inhalation – sit over a bowl of boiling water with a towel over your head and breathe in the steam – the steam will help to clear blocked nostrils
- Avoid irritants such as tobacco smoke and strong chemical odours, which may increase sinus problems

- Keep use of central heating to a minimum, dry air will dry out your nostrils

Reflexology Treatment
- Face area
- Sinuses
- Adrenals – to reduce inflammation
- Eyes
- Ears

Face (left foot): Finger-walk the front of the big toe:
- Use your right index finger to walk down the front of the big toe, from the tip to the base, until the whole of the area has been covered.

Sinuses (left foot): Walk down the centre and two sides of the small toes:
- Starting at the top of each toe using very small steps thumb-walk down to the base of each toe, or even both together.
- When treating the sides you may use your thumb or index finger, or both together.

Musculoskeletal Problems

Reflexology has been enormously successful in providing relief for all muscular and skeletal conditions. It can provide pain relief, improve mobility, reduce inflammation and dispel toxins from the system. Sufferers find that they can often reduce the analgesics they have to take with regular reflexology.

It is interesting that stiffness in the foot represents stiffness in the body. As the feet are massaged so the muscles relax and the joints become more mobile.

Arthritis

Osteoarthritis is the result of wear and tear of the joints and affects all of us to some extent, particularly in later life. In people affected

by osteoarthritis, the cartilage (connective tissue) between their bones gradually wastes away, leading to painful rubbing of bone on bone in the joints. The most frequently affected joints are in the hands, spine, knees and hips.

Causes Osteoarthritis often develops in people who are over 50 years of age. However, it can develop at any age as a result of an injury or another joint-related condition, in summary the causes are:
• Getting older
• Trauma to joints

Aboive Regular yoga sessions can help to improve mobility and relieve muscle pain.

Lifestyle Adjustments (to reduce muscle pain and increase mobility) There is no cure for arthritis but there are a number of treatments that can help slow down the condition's progress, including drug treatment and physical therapy. The list below can help to reduce the progress and symptoms of the condition:
• Regular gentle exercise such as yoga or Tai Chi
• Eating a healthy diet, since highly processed foods can lead to a build-up of toxic waste

Reflexology Treatment

The whole foot should be worked as it is a general body condition. The following reflex points, however, should be emphasised.

- Kidneys – to eliminate waste materials that accumulate around joints
- Adrenals – to fight inflammation and give pain relief
- Solar plexus – to release tension (plus any joints that are affected)

Solar Plexus (right foot): Applying pressure to this area encourages a state of relaxation:

- Place your thumbs onto the solar plexus reflex on each foot.
- Press very gently and slowly several times.

Adrenals (left foot): Rotate adrenal gland:

- Hold the left foot in the left hand and right foot with the right hand. Place your thumb on the adrenal point, located midway between the diaphragm and the waistline.
- Use your left hand to flex the foot and rotate the foot around the thumb.

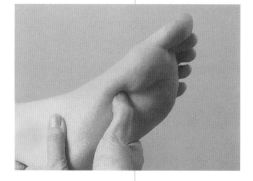

127

General Aches and Pains

Where there are problems with the muscles and joints the painful areas should be treated as described below.

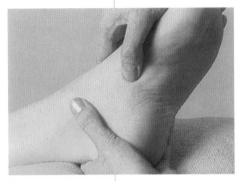

Spine

Backache (left foot)

• Caterpillar-walk down the length of the spine, with particular concentration on the affected area, e.g. cervical, thoracic, or lumbar. Repeat walking up the foot.

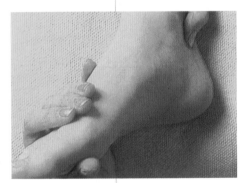

Sciatic line

Sciatica (right foot)

• Spine (as above).

• Sciatic line: thumb-walk down the Achilles tendon area on the inside of the foot across the hard heel pad and up the Achilles tendon on the outside of foot. Knuckle heel pad on sole of the foot.

Shoulder Pain e.g. Frozen shoulder (left foot)

• Shoulder area: Gently circle your thumb over the tender area several times. The shoulder reflex on the bony prominence at the base of the little toe is likely to need attention.

Shoulder area

Hip Pain (right foot)

• Hip and knee area: Hold the toes of the right foot with your right hand and with your left thumb caterpillar-walk vertically up the outer edge of the foot from the heel area up to the little toe.

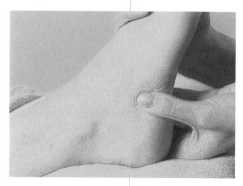

Hip/Knee area

Neck Pain

• Rotate the big toe
• Circle your thumb over the neck reflex

Also

• Work the adrenal reflex for pain relief and to reduce inflammation.
• Treat the top of the big toe (brain area) to block pain to stimulate the release of endorphins, which inhibit the transmission of pain impulses.

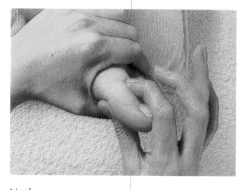

Neck area

Respiratory Problems

All respiratory problems, including simple coughs and colds, asthma, bronchitis, emphysema and other chronic bronchial conditions respond well to the regular use of reflexology. Since allergies and colds share symptoms: sneezing, runny nose, congestion and fatigue, you can't always know for certain which is ailing you. While colds are caused by hundreds of different viruses, allergies appear to be triggered by environmental factors.

Asthma

Asthma is becoming more prevalent particularly among children. It is normally characterised by wheezing and tightness in the chest due to inflammation of air passages in the lungs, causing narrowing of the airways and reducing airflow in and out of the lungs.

Causes There is no single cause of asthma, but certain factors may increase the likelihood of developing it. These include genetic factors and the environment:
• Allergies such as pollen, house dust, fur, feathers, certain foods or pollutants
• Stress and anxiety may precipitate an attack

Above Breathing exercises can help to reduce the symptoms of asthma.

Lifestyle Adjustments (to ease the symptoms of asthma) Asthma has no cure. Even when you feel fine, you still have the disease and it can flare up at any time, but you can take an active role in managing it. For successful, thorough and ongoing treatment, build strong partnerships with your doctor and other health care providers.
• Avoid dairy foods, which increase mucus production
• Breathing exercises should be practised daily (see below)

Most asthmatics breathe primarily from the chest, while the lower portion of the lungs, which should be supplying 80 percent of the oxygen, is not used. Either sit up or lie down with one hand on your abdomen and one hand on your chest. Breathe in for approximately six counts and feel your abdomen fill with air and finally your chest. Hold the breath for two counts and then breathe out for six counts. The hand on the abdomen will move before the hand on the chest if you are performing this exercise properly.

Reflexology Treatment
- Lung/chest area
- Solar plexus/diaphragm – to release tension
- Adrenal glands – for allergies

Lung/chest area: Thumb-walk the chest area from the diaphragm line to the shoulder girdle line on the sole of the foot:
- Pull the toes back slightly with the left hand, with the fingers cupped over the front of the toes.
- Start at the base of the toes, and use your right thumb to caterpillar-walk in vertical strips from the diaphragm line to the shoulder girdle line.

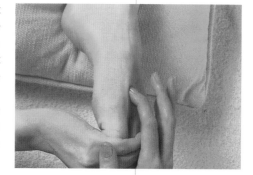

Solar plexus/diaphragm: Applying pressure to this area encourages a state of relaxation:
- Place your thumbs onto the solar plexus reflex on each foot.
- Press very gently and slowly several times.

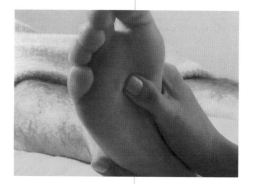

Above Colds are a common problem and while there is no cure you can relieve the symptoms.

Coughs/Colds/Respiratory Infections

We all occasionally get a cold and reflexology is an excellent way of relieving many of the symptoms and aiding the removal of mucus to prevent the occurrence of more serious conditions. Most coughs and colds are caused by viruses. Many different viruses can infect the nose and throat. They are passed on when the virus is coughed and sneezed into the air. Coughing is the body's way of removing foreign material or mucus from the lungs and upper airway passages or of reacting to an irritated airway. The common symptoms are a cough and a runny nose, in addition there may be a raised temperature (fever), a sore throat, headache, tiredness and loss of appetite. A build-up of mucus behind the eardrums may cause dulled hearing or mild earache. If symptoms persist consult a doctor.

Causes A cough is only a symptom, not a disease, and is generally caused by:
- Exposure to viruses – schoolchildren have more coughs and colds due to exposure to lots of different germs and close proximity to each other
- Nasal discharge
- Infection

Lifestyle Adjustments (to treat and prevent coughs and colds) There's no quick way of getting rid of a cough that's caused by a viral infection. It will usually clear up after your immune system has fought off the virus, so the list below shows ways to boost your immune system so you can fight off coughs and colds:
- Eat garlic, which is known as nature's antibiotic
- Hot spices such as ginger will help to break down phlegm
- Take vitamin C daily – at least one dose
- Eat foods that are rich in zinc, vitamin E and Omega-3 fatty acids as these all help to boost the immune system

Reflexology Treatment
- Lung/chest area – to break up congestion
- Nose
- Throat
- Eyes
- Ears
- Thymus – to boost the immune system
- Lymph drainage – especially upper lymphatics

Thymus: Move your thumb to the right almost as far as the inside of the foot and use your thumb to circle over the thymus area.

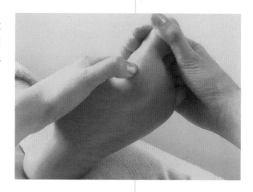

Lymph drainage: Gently squeeze webbing between each of the toes. This area can be quite sensitive. Remember if you find a tender area, gently massage it in a circular direction.

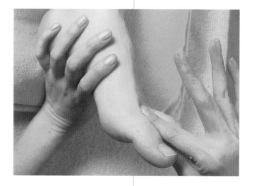

Skin Problems

Your skin is the largest organ of the body and it protects you from bacteria and viruses that can cause infections. It also helps you sense the outside world, such as whether it is hot or cold, and regulates your body temperature. Conditions that irritate, clog or inflame your skin can cause symptoms such as redness, swelling, burning and itching. Many skin problems also affect your appearance. Skin disorders include acne, eczema, dermatitis and psoriasis. Reflexology can help any skin condition – it improves circulation and so the skin should take on a healthy glow.

Causes Allergies, irritants, your genetic makeup and some diseases and immune system problems can cause skin problems, including:
- Hormonal imbalances
- Dietary factors
- Stress

Lifestyle Adjustments (to treat and prevent skin problems) The skin reflects and reacts to imbalances within the body's internal landscape and the effects of the environment. Internal disharmonies caused by strong emotions, diet and your constitution, as well as environmental influences, all contribute to the development of a skin disorder. The list below may help to reduce your symptoms:
- Avoid sugar, fatty foods and caffeine
- Eat plenty of fruit and vegetables
- Drink six to eight glasses of water daily
- Avoid stress
- Never wear man-made fibres, such as nylon, next to the skin
- Avoid over-exposure to the sun as this will aggravate any symptoms you already have
- Hydration – keep the skin moisturised and lubricated (not applicable for acne)
- Consult your doctor for support and advice on chronic conditions

Reflexology Treatment

A complete treatment is beneficial to stimulate the elimination of toxins, but special attention should be given to the following areas:

- Reflex zones relating to the area affected e.g. the face
- Pituitary gland – to regulate hormonal activity
- Kidneys – to improve elimination
- Adrenal glands – to counteract inflammation
- Lymphatics – to cleanse the body

Face (left foot): Finger-walk the front of the big toe:

- Use your right index finger to walk down the front of the big toe, from the tip to the base, until the whole of the area has been covered.

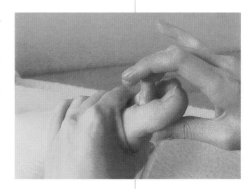

Pituitary gland (right foot): Hook-in and back-up on the centre of the big toe:

- Place the fingers of your left hand over the front of the toes and your thumb under the back of the toes. Using the hook-in and back-up technique, press the pituitary gland with the corner of your right thumb.

135

Self-Reflexology

Whilst self-treatment is possible, it is virtually impossible to give yourself a complete treatment of foot reflexology. It is difficult to be able to relax sufficiently to derive the maximum benefit from a treatment. It is also very awkward to reach some of the reflex points.

When carrying out self-administration there is not the exchange of energy which exists when one individual works on another. Therefore, it is much more relaxing and therapeutic to entrust your feet to the hands of another. However, it is possible to treat a limited number of specific reflexes to relieve ailments such as headaches. So self-treatment can be very useful to achieve quick relief from a condition.

When you work on your own feet sit down as comfortably as possible and surround yourself with plenty of pillows.

You need to be able to sit cross-legged or at least be able to raise one foot on to the opposite knee so that you can see what you are treating. You may either sit on the floor, on a bed, or on a chair.

The sequence on the page opposite is excellent for de-stressing yourself and for general health care. It should take about ten minutes and can be done whenever you feel like it.

Step 1 Stroke the Foot to Relax

1. Using both hands, stroke the foot, working upward from the toes towards the ankle bones ...

2. ... and back again

Step 2 Finger-walk the Solar Plexus to Release Stress and Tension

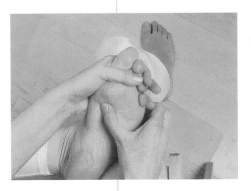

1. Wrap your fingers and thumb around the ball of the foot with your holding hand. Thumb-walk across the diaphragm line with your other hand.

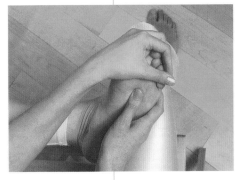

2. When you reach the solar plexus, press gently into it, then gradually release the pressure.

Step 3 The Spine

1. Stroke gently down the inside of the foot with the heel of your hand to encourage the spine to relax.

2. Caterpillar-walk up the inside of the foot, working from the base of the heel up to the base of the big toe nail. You may walk in the other direction if you prefer. Pay particular attention to any areas that are sore.

Step 4 The Neck

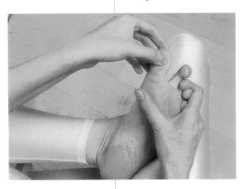

1. Hold the big toe between your index finger and thumb and gently rotate it clockwise and anticlockwise to release tension and increase movement in the neck.

2. Thumb-walk across the back of the base of the big toe and continue to walk across the front base of the big toe.

Step 5 The Pituitary Gland

Locate the widest part of the big toe and the pituitary gland is found approximately at the mid-point of this line.

Step 6 Chest and Colon Booster

Make a fist with your hand and place it on the fleshy area of the ball of the foot. Use a gentle, circular motion on the upper third of the foot to relax and decongest that chest area.

You may work on the lower third of the foot to encourage elimination from the colon. This is excellent for constipation.

Step 7 Special Focus

Treat any areas which need special attention. Here the kidney area is illustrated, but other common areas to come back to include the head and brain area if you have a headache and the stomach area if you have indigestion. Please refer to the relevant chapter for advice on treating specific ailments.

Step 8 And Finally ...

Stroke the foot again to disperse any toxins which have been released.

Repeat the sequence on the other foot. Now allow yourself time to sit or lie back for at least 10–15 minutes.

Taking Care of Your Feet

Most us are fortunate enough to be born with a healthy pair of feet, but by the time we reach old age (and often before!) we have developed some kind of foot disorder. What is more, it is probably self-induced, perhaps caused by years of ill-fitting, fashionable shoes. Feet are often the most neglected part of the body, but now it is time to learn to take care of your feet. Not only will they look good but you will also feel much more healthy. If you bear in mind that every part of the foot represents a part of the body in miniature, you should look at any corns, calluses and athlete's foot in a new light. Is that athlete's foot between toes two and three affecting your eyes? Was that corn on the top of toe four there before or after you got that toothache? No wonder your neck has been playing up – look at the redness at the base of your big toe. Perhaps you should be kinder and more considerate to your feet.

Remember:

- Walk around barefoot as often as possible. Feet do not like to be confined in shoes all the time. This will help to prevent foot deformities.
- Always cut your toenails straight across to stop ingrowing toenails from occurring.
- Use a pumice stone on the hardened areas to remove dead skin and prevent build-up.
- Massage your feet regularly with pure, organic foot creams. You may use high-quality pure essential oils for their healing properties. Try to avoid chemical foot sprays.
- Throw your shoes off at the weekend and walk on the grass or the beach. This will make you feel grounded yet exhilarated.
- Avoid socks that are made of synthetic fibres such as nylon, which make the feet perspire. Wear cotton and wool socks instead.
- Exercise your feet regularly to keep yourself supple and healthy.

Foot Care Tips

Wash your feet daily to remove bacteria and dry thoroughly, particularly between the toes. This will help to prevent fungal conditions such as athlete's foot from developing and also stops your feet from becoming smelly. You may like to add pure essential oils to your footbaths. Add six drops of essential oil to a bowl of hand-hot water just before you immerse the feet and soak for about 10–15 minutes.

Athlete's Foot
3 drops lavender
3 drops myrrh

Immune Booster
3 drops lemon
3 drops tea tree

Tired, Swollen Feet
3 drops chamomile
3 drops lavender

Restorative After a Long, Hard Day
2 drops lavender
2 drops peppermint
2 drops rosemary

To Stimulate Circulation
2 drops geranium
2 drops black pepper
2 drops mandarin

Cracked or Chapped Feet
3 drops benzoin
3 drops patchouli

Cooling Foot Cream
To 30g cream add:
7 drops peppermint

Cracked Foot Cream
To 30g cream add:
3 drops benzoin
2 drops myrrh
2 drops patchouli

Try These Simple Exercises Every Day

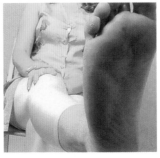 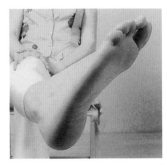

1. Rotate your feet in both directions to loosen them up and get rid of unwanted fluid around the ankles.

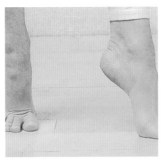 

2. Walk on the balls of your feet – especially if you have chest problems such as asthma.

3. Pick up a pencil with your toes. This helps to tone up ligaments and tendons and also helps relax the neck and shoulder muscles.

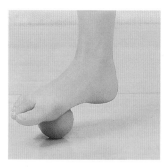

4. Place a ball under your foot and roll it the length of your foot. This will stimulate the respiratory and the digestive systems.

5. Walk on the outsides of your feet to keep them from rolling inwards.

Hand
Reflexology

Introduction to Hand Reflexology

Hand reflexology involves applying pressure through the fingers and thumbs to the reflex areas of the hands. These reflex areas are found on all parts of the hands and they correspond to the organs, glands and structures of the body. The hands can be seen as a mirror of the body, the right hand reflecting the right-hand side of the body while the left hand reflects the left-hand side.

Reflexology is a simple, non-invasive natural therapy, which stimulates the inner healing forces within the body, bringing about physical, mental and emotional well-being. Whether you have a specific health problem or are just looking for a way to relieve tension and promote optimum health, reflexology is of excellent therapeutic value to everyone.

Hand reflexology is completely safe, provided that it is administered correctly. As long as a particular reflex is not overworked there is no danger of over-stimulation, which can cause excessive elimination and unpleasant side-effects. It can be used on everyone, from young babies to the very elderly.

Above Reflex points in the hand mirror specific organs and structures of the body.

Why Hand Reflexology?

Foot reflexology is the most popular form of reflexology and if you make an appointment to see a professional reflexologist the treatment would take place primarily on the feet. Hand reflexology is usually recommended as a self-help treatment to reinforce the work of the reflexologist.

However, times are changing and there is an increasing interest in the use of hand reflexology as the primary treatment. It has often been found that hand reflexology is a highly effective treatment, and sometimes patients have responded more quickly to hand reflexology than to foot reflexology. The best practices today generally use a combination of hand and foot reflexology and the results are excellent.

There are some occasions when it is impossible to administer foot reflexology, and then working the hands becomes a necessity. Such circumstances include:

- If the foot is injured – e.g. fractures, sprains etc.
- If the foot is infected.
- If the foot has been amputated.
- If a person is too shy or embarrassed to expose his/her feet.
- If the feet are extremely sensitive and cannot be touched without causing discomfort.
- If the foot, or part of the foot, is very inflamed – e.g. with gout in the big toe.
- If foot reflexology has not previously worked, or progress is very slow.
- If self-treatment is required.

The Bony Structure of the Hands

Each hand and wrist is made up of 27 bones. They are:

Eight carpals (wrist bones) arranged in two rows. They are known as the trapezium (four-sided), trapezoid (four-sided), capitate, hamate (hook-shaped), scaphoid (like a boat), lunate (resembles a crescent moon), triquetral and pisiform (pea-shaped).

Five metacarpals, which form the palm of the hand. The heads of these bones make the knuckles.

Fourteen phalanges, which are the finger and thumb bones. The thumb has two phalanges, whereas the fingers have three.

The bones of the hand and wrist are held in place by a large number of muscles, tendons and ligaments. There is a rich supply of nerve endings in the hands, which make them very sensitive.

Right The main bones in the hand.

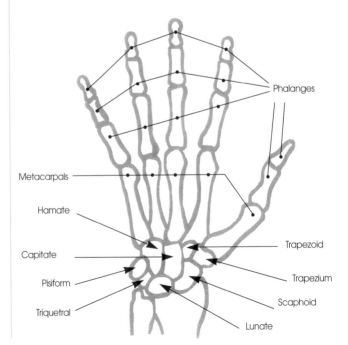

Phalanges

Metacarpals

Hamate

Capitate

Pisiform

Triquetral

Trapezoid

Trapezium

Scaphoid

Lunate

Principles of Reflexology

Ten Longitudinal Zones

According to reflexology, the body can be divided into ten longitudinal zones, which run the length of body from the tips of the toes to the head and out to the fingertips and vice versa. If an imaginary line is drawn through the centre of the body there are five zones to the right of this mid-line and five zones to the left.

Zone one runs from the big toe, up the leg and centre of the body to the head and then down to the thumb.

Zone two runs from the second toe up to the head and then down to the index finger.

Zone three extends from the third toe up to the head, then down to the third finger and so on.

All organs and parts of the body that lie within the same zone are related to each other. If any part of a zone is stimulated in the hand this will affect the entire zone throughout the body.

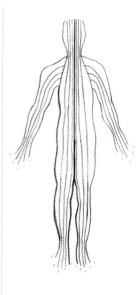

Above The ten longitudinal zones.

Left The reflex zones in the hands.

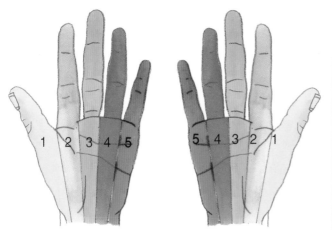

151

The Transverse Zones

Reflexology also divides the hands (and feet) into transverse or horizontal sections.

- The first transverse zone – the diaphragm line – on the hand is located just below the padded area beneath the fingers. All the organs above the diaphragm on the body are found here.
- The second transverse zone – waist line – runs from the base of the web between the thumb and index finger, where the thumb joins the hand across the hand.
- The third transverse zone – pelvic line – circles the wrist. The transverse zones and the longitudinal zones help us to describe the position of the reflexes on the hands.

Below The transverse zones of the hands.

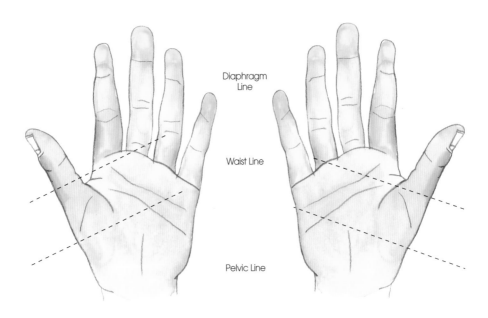

Diaphragm Line

Waist Line

Pelvic Line

Getting Started

Setting up as a reflexologist is reasonably straightforward, and working just on the hands is easier as you do not have to provide as much privacy. You simply need a private space that is warm, welcoming and comfortable. It is important that the receiver remains as calm and relaxed as possible, so healing can be facilitated.

Creating a Suitable Atmosphere

The beauty of giving a hand reflexology treatment is that it can be carried out anywhere, but if you create the right ambience in your own healing space, you will achieve optimum results.

Ideally the surroundings should be as peaceful and calm as

Above The gentle scent of potpourri can enhance the atmosphere.

possible. Telephones ringing and children banging on the door to attract your attention are not conducive to relaxation, so be sure to remove as many distractions as possible. Some people enjoy silence during their treatment while others will prefer to listen to some soft relaxation music. It is up to the individual, so be sure to check with them before you start.

The room should be warm and inviting with soft and subdued lighting. Essential oils can be burned prior to the treatment. Particularly relaxing oils include lavender, chamomile, frankincense, sandalwood and ylang ylang. A vase of fresh flowers or some softly scented potpourri will also enhance the environment.

Positions for Working

Correct positioning of the receiver is an important factor in the success of your treatment. Whatever position you choose it is vital that it affords complete relaxation for both you and the receiver.

154

A professional reflexologist will undoubtedly have a massage couch. It is not essential for you to purchase one, although you may decide to invest in one later on.

You may decide to work with the receiver lying on a bed. You need to place pillows under the head to support the neck, and to enable you to observe any facial expressions. Pillows can also be placed under the receiver's knees for comfort, and it is a good idea to position a pillow under the hand you are about to treat. This provides a comfortable working position for you to work from. You will sit to one side, facing the receiver. Towels or blankets are essential to cover the receiver. This not only makes the receiver feel safe and secure, but it also counteracts the loss of body heat which will occur as the treatment progresses.

You may prefer to work on the floor and this is also acceptable. You will need a well-padded surface, which can be made by placing a thick duvet, some blankets or sleeping bags on the floor. As before, for the receiver's comfort place pillows under the head and under the knees and cover them. Put a pillow under your knees for your own comfort and a pillow under the hand which you are treating first.

Some reflexologists work with the receiver sitting on a chair with their hand resting on a stool or table at the side, but this position is not always comfortable and can encourage conversation. Another possibility is to sit facing the receiver with their hand resting on a pillow on a table or bench.

Above A massage couch is a useful purchase for frequent treatments, but it is not essential.

Below Left If using a couch or bed, ensure the receiver is warm and comfortable.

Below Facing the receiver across a table or bench is a simple and effective reflexology position.

Other Points to Remember:

- Have extra towels/blankets on hand just in case the receiver feels cold.
- Remove all jewellery from your hands to avoid scratching.
- Ask the receiver to remove his/her jewellery so that the treatment is not impeded.
- Any restrictive clothing such as ties and belts may be loosened to maximise comfort.
- Clip your nails closely to avoid them digging in.
- Check that your nails are clean!
- Wash your hands prior to a treatment.
- Do not use oils or creams during the reflexology session. Lubricants make it difficult to hold the receiver's hands properly, cause your fingers and thumbs to slip and decrease your sensitivity. You may use them at the end of the reflexology sequence.

Below left A visual examination of the hands is essential before starting a treatment.

Below right
A deviated index finger may signify sinus problems.

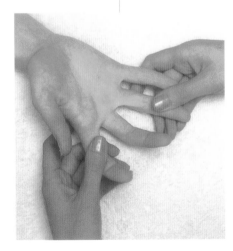

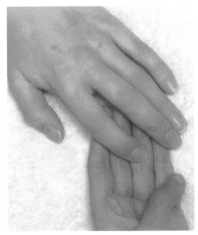

Examining the Hands

Prior to starting your treatment it is very enlightening to examine the hands visually. You will be amazed at what they can reveal. A healthy person will have hands that are a good colour, with unblemished skin and good muscle tone. The hands should feel pleasantly warm but not excessively moist and clammy. Nails should have a strong and healthy appearance. Here are some things to look out for:

- Infections of the hands and nails
- Calluses and hard skin
- Thin skin
- Blisters
- Cracks and crevices
- Warts
- Scars
- Cuts
- Spots and rashes
- Colour – too pale, too red, yellow, purple, or mottled.
- Nails – split, flaked, broken. Are they hardened, thickened, ridged, spotted, or a peculiar shape? (Spoon-shaped nails are sometimes seen in iron-deficiency anaemia)
- Shape of the fingers and thumbs – are they bent or straight and/ or puffy?

Any of these abnormalities indicate an imbalance of a reflex zone or zones. It is not relevant what the abnormality is – what is important is the site. For instance if there is a wart or some hard skin located on the outer aspect of the thumb this could indicate that there is a neck problem.

Puffiness around the wrist would indicate an imbalance of the lymphatic system as the pelvic lymphatic reflex area is located around the wrist. You will now look at your hands in a new light (see opposite).

Hand Relaxation Techniques

The first contact between your hands and the receiver's hands is very important. Use relaxation techniques to help you to put both of you at ease and build up a sense of trust.

Above Creams and oils should only be used after treatment.

If you use these techniques, you will find that it feels very natural to work on someone's hands, and any initial nervousness and hesitation will disappear. These techniques will be enjoyable for both of you. As your confidence grows you can be creative and develop your own new techniques. Any movements that feel good to you will feel wonderful to the receiver.

Relaxation techniques should always begin and end a hand reflexology treatment. You will need to spend about ten minutes at the beginning of a session and a few minutes at the end on these. You can also include a few during your reflexology procedure. Perform all the relaxation techniques on one hand before moving onto the other hand.

Ideally no creams or oils should be used for your preliminary relaxation sequence, otherwise when you try to carry out the reflexology procedure the hands will be too slippery to apply sufficient pressure to the reflexology points. However, at the end of the treatment a small amount of oil or cream can be used. If the hands do feel at all greasy at the end of the relaxation session then just wipe them gently with a towel.

If you do not have time to give a hand reflexology treatment then this relaxation routine on its own can be very beneficial. Our hands are in constant use throughout the day and they really appreciate a massage! Massage them every day with creams or oil to thoroughly moisturise the skin and keep them soft and smooth. A hand massage can be given any time, any place, anywhere. Before you start remember to remove all watches and jewellery.

Greeting the Hands

This initial contact will help to relax and reassure the receiver. Take hold of the receiver's right hand between both of your hands and gently clasp it for a few minutes Work with your eyes closed to heighten your sensitivity. Try to become aware of any tension and imagine it flowing out through your hands.

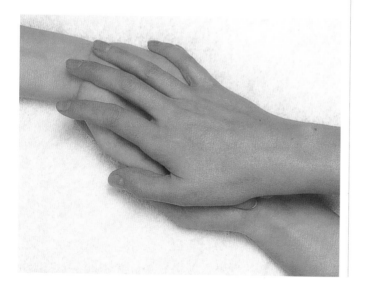

Stroking the Hands and Lower Arm

The receiver will experience a deep sense of well-being and relaxation as the nerves are soothed and the tension melts away. You will feel the hand warm up as you help to stimulate the circulation and aid the elimination of toxins.

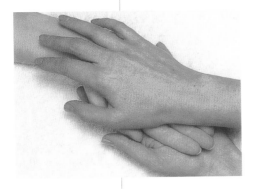

1. Support the forearm with your left hand and gently stroke up the hand and arm with your right hand.

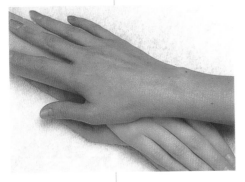

2. As you reach the elbow, glide lightly back but do not exert pressure down the arm and hand.

Stroking the Hands (Effleurage)

For a deeper movement, stroke the palm with the heel of your hand.

1. Supporting the receiver's right wrist with your left hand, stroke up to the top of the hand only. Repeat this movement several times.

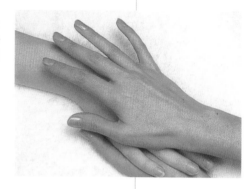

2. Now turn the receiver's hand over and repeat on the palm of their hand.

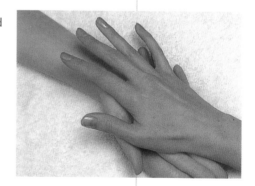

161

Opening The Hands

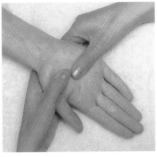 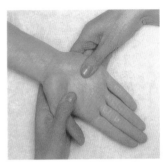

1. Take the right hand in both of yours, with the palm uppermost. Start at the wrist with your thumbs parallel and touching in the centre of the palm.

2. Slide your thumbs out to the side, gently opening up the palm of the hand. Repeat this movement in rows until you reach the base of the fingers.

 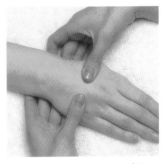

3. Turn the hand over and repeat the movements in steps 1 and 2 on the top of the hand.

Working the Palm of the Hand

You can work quite firmly into the palm of the hand. If your own hands are not very flexible then try the next technique.

1. With the palm uppermost, interlock your little fingers with the receiver's right hand – one with the little finger, one with the thumb.

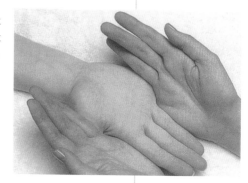

2. Bring your thumbs round onto the palm and work into the palm with small, round, outward circular movements.

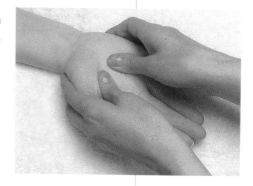

163

Knuckling the Palm of the Hand

Make a fist with your right hand and support the receiver's hand, palm uppermost, with your other hand. Work into the palm of their hand with circular movements using your knuckles. This movement helps to loosen muscles, joints and tendons. It also increases the flexibility of your own hands.

Stroking Between the Bones

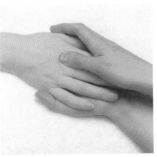 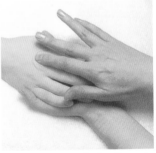

1. Hold the receiver's hand with one hand to give support. Use the thumb of your free hand to work along each of the furrows between the bones of the hand. Start between the knuckles and stroke down towards the wrist.

2. Now use your index finger to perform the same movement.

Loosening the Wrist

1. Support the hand with your fingers. Use your thumbs to work in small circles all around the inside of the wrist.

2. Now turn the hand over and work in the same way on the other side of the wrist

Moving the Wrist

1. Interlock your fingers with the receiver's and then bend the wrist slowly and gently, first forwards.

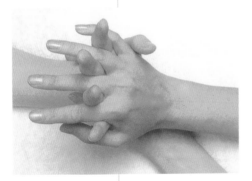

2. Now bend it backwards.

3. Then bend the wrist from side to side.

4. Finally, rotate clockwise and anticlockwise.

167

Wrist Rolling

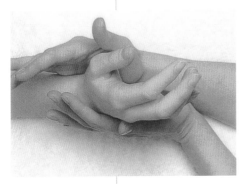

1. This technique is highly invigorating. Leave the upper arm on the couch and lift up the forearm. Place your palms on the sides of your partner's wrist. Move your hands rapidly back and forth. Your partner's hand should flop and move loosely as you perform this movement.

2. If you prefer you may slot your thumbs in between the thumbs and little finger to perform this movement.

Stretch and Squeeze the Fingers and Thumb

Hold your partner's wrist to support the hand. Gently and slowly stretch and squeeze each finger individually, working from the knuckle to the tip.

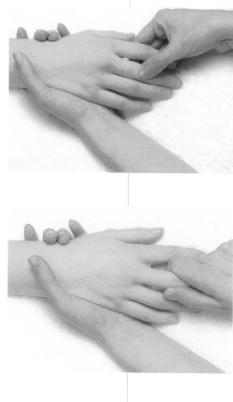

Loosen the Fingers and Thumb

Make circular pressures around each joint, using your thumb and index finger.

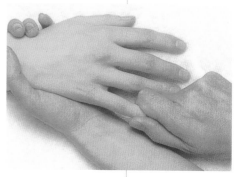

Bending the Fingers and Thumb

1. Gently flex and extend each finger and thumb joint with your thumb and index finger. (There are two joints in the thumb, three in the fingers).

 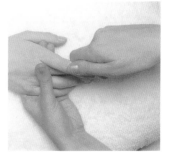

2. Circle the thumb and fingers individually, both clockwise

3. Now circle them both anticlockwise.

Solar Plexus Release

To release any remaining tension place your thumb on the solar plexus reflex, which is found almost in the centre of the palm and press slowly and gently into it.

Fingertip Stroking

To end your relaxation routine, sandwich your partner's hand between your palm and, using your fingertips, stroke the hand slowly from the wrist to the tips.

Now practise all these relaxation techniques on the other hand.

171

Basic Hand Reflexology Techniques

The basic techniques you need to learn in order to practise hand reflexology are very easy to become expert in. You just need to familiarise yourself with them before you take on your first receiver. It is a good idea to practise on friends and family first – until you become proficient.

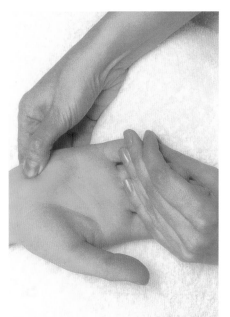

Now that you have mastered the relaxation techniques, you are going to learn how to treat the reflex areas in the hand. The reflex points are tiny and the thumb is the main tool used for applying pressure, although on certain areas of the hand the fingers are used.

Please note the following before you begin:
• Keep fingernails short – a nail digging into the skin is very painful.
• Both you and the receiver should remove all watches, bracelets and rings.
• Use only the flat pads of your fingers and thumbs to prevent even short nails from scratching or digging in.
• Do not apply too much pressure – reflexology should not be uncomfortable.
• As stated previously, do not use oil or cream on the receiver's hands for the preliminary relaxation movements or for the step-by-step procedure. If the hands are sticky or slippery then you will not be able to make good contact with the reflex points. Oils and creams may be used for the final relaxation movements.

Holding Technique

It is very important to support the hands properly during the treatment, so that you have full control and exude an air of confidence. You also need to be able to reach and pinpoint the reflex zones easily and effectively.

Never grip the hand that you are working on too tightly or pull the skin taut, otherwise your receiver will feel tense and uncomfortable.

Remember to place a pillow under the receiver's hand, which should be covered with a towel to protect it if you are intending to use oils at the end of the session.

Stroke gently down the inside of the hand with the heel of your hand, to encourage the spine to relax.

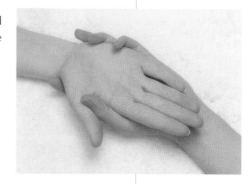

If you are working on the top (dorsal side), hold the hand by supporting the wrist from underneath in a 'handshake' position.

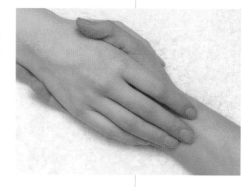

Checklist

- Do not dig in with your nails.
- Bend the first joint of the thumb only.
- Bend the thumb slightly – it should be neither too bent or too straight.
- Take very small steps.
- Movements are always forward never backward.
- Pressure should be steady.
- Pressure should be firm, yet not hard enough to induce pain.

Thumb-walking/Caterpillar-walking Technique

This technique is used for working large areas of the hand. Place the flat pad part of your thumb on the area to be treated, bend the first joint slightly and then unbend the thumb slightly so that you move forward a little.

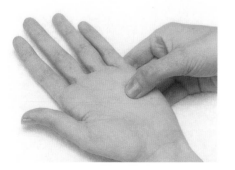

1. Continue in this way, moving forward in tiny creeping movements like a caterpillar, without losing contact with the hand. It is impossible to walk with a straight thumb and if you bend the thumb too much your nail will dig into the skin. Try out this technique on the palm of your own hand first.

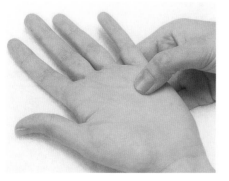

2. While your thumb is walking, your other fingers should rest gently around the hand. Try to maintain a constant and even pressure, always working in a forward direction. Do not worry if your movements feel somewhat jerky and clumsy at first. Persevere and you will achieve a smooth, consistent pressure.

Thumb too arched (incorrect).

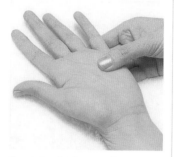

Thumb too flat (incorrect).

Pressure Circles

Pressure circles may be performed with the pad of the thumb or a finger. They can be used for working specific reflex points or to relieve the sensitivity of tender reflexes.

Place your thumb or finger on to a reflex point and press gently into the area. Keeping this pressure constant, circle gently over the point several times.

Left Pressure circles on the kidney point.

175

Checklist

- Maintain a steady, even pressure.
- Move only in a forward direction.
- Take care not to dig your nails in.
- Take only very small steps.
- Use very gentle pressure – finger-walking is specifically designed for bony and sensitive areas.

Finger-walking Technique

The finger-walking technique is almost the same as thumb-walking. The object is the same – to exert a constant steady pressure, which is comfortable and effective for the receiver. Use finger-walking in preference to thumb-walking on bony or sensitive areas, such as the top surface of the hand.

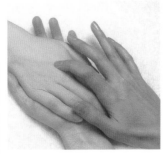

1. Practise single finger-walking first. Place the tip of your index finger on the area to be treated. Bend the first joint of the finger slightly and then unbend it a little, to move the fingertip in a forward direction. Try this technique on the back of the hand, walking from the knuckles towards your wrist and remember to take the smallest possible steps.

2. Now try multiple finger-walking using two or more fingers, once again working down the top surface of the hand. If you are working on top of the hand walking downward, place your fist under the palm of the hand to support it. Practise with one, two, or three fingers to see which is most comfortable for you and the receiver.

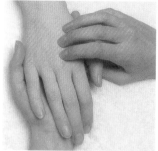

You may also work sideways across the top (dorsal surface) of the hand. When working sideways your thumb will be placed under the palm of the hand to support it while your fingers walk across the top.

Press and Release

This technique is particularly effective for relieving pain and you may perform it with either your thumb or finger. Press into a tender point for several seconds (here the ovary is illustrated).

Release the pressure and repeat several times until the sensitivity decreases.

Left Press and release on the ovary area.

177

Rotation on a Point

1. This technique involves pinpointing an area to be treated and rotating the hand around it. Thus the term – 'rotation on a point'. Place the pad of your thumb or finger on the relevant reflex point. (Here the right ovary is illustrated.)

2. Use your other hand to rotate the receiver's hand around the point several times.

Hook-in and Back-up

To access specific points requiring greater accuracy, this technique is excellent. It would never be used for covering a large area – thumb- or finger-walking would be much more appropriate.

Press your thumb into your chosen point and apply pressure (hook-in) and then pull back across the point (back-up).

Hand Reflexology for Common Ailments

As with foot reflexology (see p104) this section looks at some common ailments and suggests areas to concentrate on. Many of the

Adrenals: Hook-in and back-up.

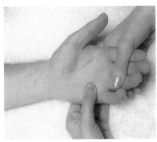

Diaphragm: Pressure circles.

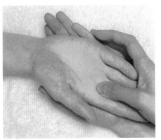

Eyes: Pressure circles.

Face: Thumb- or finger-walk.

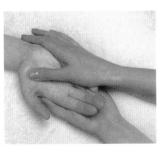

Kidneys: Pressure circles.

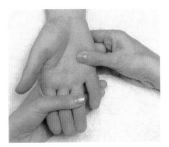

Ears: Pressure circles.

180

areas shown below feature in most of the recommended treatments. Other treatment areas specific to individual ailments are illustrated throughout this section.

In the course of a hand reflexology treatment, disorders may show up as tender areas. Once you are familiar with the Basic Hand Reflexology Treatments (pp172-179) use the techniques indicated below to treat specific areas.

Liver: Thumb-walk.

Lung/Chest Area: Thumb-walk.

Lymphatics (Groin): Squeeze the webbing between fingers.

Pituitary gland: Hook-in and back–up.

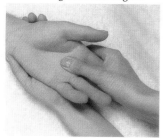

Solar Plexus: Pressure circles.

Spine: Caterpillar-walk inside the thumb.

181

Digestive Problems

Constipation

Constipation is commonly caused by a diet low in fibre; inadequate intake of water; lack of exercise; anxiety and excessive use of certain medications such as laxatives, which make the bowel lazy; painkillers and antibiotics. It is characterised by the infrequent passage of hard stools, usually with some discomfort.

Indigestion/Heartburn

This is a very common problem, giving symptoms of a taste of acid in the mouth and pain in the chest, sometimes with nausea. It is caused by eating the wrong foods such as cakes, biscuits, fatty foods, spicy foods, rich foods or dairy foods. Rushing when eating or not chewing food properly and stress will also exacerbate acidity.

Lifestyle Adjustments (to reduce constipation, indigestion, or heartburn) Dietary and lifestyle changes can regulate the gastrointestinal tract, reducing the likelihood of these ailments.

- Avoid stressful situations and learn to relax
- Regular exercise also helps to keep the gastrointestinal tract working efficiently and reduces the risk of indigestion
- Chew food slowly in pleasant surroundings

Reflexology Treatment (Constipation)

- Ileocecal valve – which controls movement between the small and large intestines
- Small intestines
- Large intestines
- Adrenal glands
- Solar plexus – to reduce tension

Reflexology Treatment (Indigestion/Heartburn)

- Stomach/pancreas/duodenum
- Solar plexus – to reduce stress
- Adrenal glands – to reduce inflammation
- Liver/gallbladder – where there is nausea

Small intestines: Thumb-walk zones one to four:

- Place the flat pad part of your thumb on the area to be treated, bend the first joint slightly and then unbend the thumb slightly so that you move forward a little. Continue in this way, moving forward in tiny creeping movements like a caterpillar, without losing contact with the hand.

Stomach/pancreas/duodenum: Thumb-walk zones one to three between diaphragm line and waistline:

- Place the flat pad part of your thumb on the area to be treated, bend the first joint slightly and then unbend the thumb slightly so that you move forward a little. Continue in this way, moving forward in tiny creeping movements like a caterpillar, without losing contact with the hand.

Genito-Urinary Problems

Cystitis

This is an inflammation of the inner lining of the bladder, usually caused by an infection entering the bladder via the urethral opening. The bacteria can come from the vagina or from the intestines via the anus. The symptoms include a frequent desire to urinate, often with a burning sensation. The urine may be stained with blood and there may be a fever.

Lifestyle Adjustments (to reduce the likelihood of developing cystitis) It's not always possible to prevent cystitis, but you can take some steps to help avoid the condition:

• Some people find certain types of food and drink make their cystitis worse: for example, coffee, fruit juice or spicy foods. If you know there are foods that trigger your cystitis it's best to avoid them
• Don't wait to go if you need to urinate and always empty your bladder fully
• Drink cranberry juice
• Increase fluid intake to flush out the bladder
• Avoid using perfumed bubble bath, soap or talcum powder

Reflexology Treatment

• Bladder
• Kidneys
• Ureter tubes
• Lymphatics

N.B. Always work from the kidney to the bladder – NEVER from the bladder to the kidney – to avoid the risk of transferring a bladder infection into a kidney causing an infection, which is far more serious.

Kidneys: Pressure circles over kidney point:
- Press into a tender point for several seconds.
- Keeping this pressure constant, circle gently over the point several times.

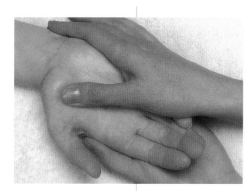

Working down the ureter tube towards the bladder: From the above position turn thumb and work down towards the inside of the hand to the bladder using the 'pressure circles' technique.

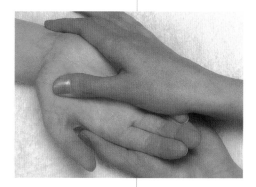

185

Menstrual Problems

Ailments falling into this category include premenstrual syndrome (PMS); painful, absent or scanty periods; menopause; fibroids in the uterus; ovarian cysts and infertility problems. Reflexology can correct hormonal imbalances, relax the body and mind, give pain relief from menstrual cramps and aid the elimination of excess fluid from the body.

Lifestyle Adjustments (to reduce the symptoms of menstrual problems) Reducing stress levels and making changes in diet and exercise may help to relieve symptoms.
• Reduce salt, which leads to fluid retention
• Reduce sugar and caffeine, which aggravate mood swings
• Increase fibre intake
• Take a vitamin B-complex supplement
• Take gentle exercise such as yoga and Tai Chi
• If menopausal symptoms increase calcium-rich foods, e.g. fish, especially sardines, sunflower, pumpkin, sesame seeds and nuts

Reflexology Treatment
• Ovaries (illustrated using index finger)
• Uterus (illustrated using thumb)
• Fallopian tubes
• Kidneys – where there is excessive fluid
• Breasts – where there is soreness
• Pituitary gland – to balance hormones
• Solar plexus – to relax
• Spine – for back pain

Ovaries: Rotate on reflex point on outside of wrist.
- Place the pad of your thumb or finger on the relevant reflex point.
- Use your other hand to rotate the receiver's hand around the point several times.

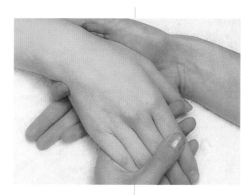

Uterus: Rotate on reflex point on inside of wrist:
- Place the pad of your thumb or finger on the relevant reflex point.
- Use your other hand to rotate the receiver's hand around the point several times.

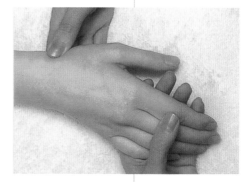

Head

Headaches/Migraine

Headaches are usually caused by stress. Problems with the vertebrae in the neck arising from old whiplash injuries or poor posture are also frequently responsible. If headaches persist then medical advice should always be sought in case there is an underlying disorder. It may well be worth consulting an osteopath for spinal realignment.

Migraines are extremely painful, one-sided headaches usually accompanied by vomiting and an aversion to bright lights. Visual disturbances are also common. Sensitivity to certain foods such as cheese, chocolate and red wine; missed meals; tiredness and hormonal imbalances may also be contributory factors.

Lifestyle Adjustments (to reduce the head and neck problems) The effectiveness of any lifestyle change in reducing your symptoms will depend on whether your neck pain is caused by activities, an injury or another medical condition. You may see an improvement by:
- Reducing your stress levels.
- If you suffer from migraine try avoiding chocolate, cheese, drinks containing caffeine, especially coffee; alcohol, especially red wine, and food additives.
- Exercise can relieve tension and loosen tight muscles.

Right Reducing the stress in your working life can help to prevent headaches.

Reflexology Treatment
- Head and brain area
- Spine, especially the neck
- Pituitary gland – to balance the hormones
- Solar plexus – to reduce stress
- Liver – to reduce nausea. The entire digestive system should be worked to encourage elimination
- Eyes

Head and brain: Thumb-walk back and sides of thumb:
- Place the flat pad part of your thumb on the area to be treated, bend the first joint slightly and then unbend the thumb slightly so that you move forward a little. Continue in this way, moving forward in tiny creeping movements like a caterpillar, without losing contact with the hand.

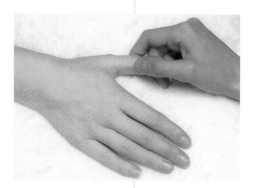

Heart Problems

Angina

Angina is caused by a lack of oxygen reaching the heart muscle due to coronary heart disease, high blood pressure or diseased heart valves. The symptoms are chest pain, which can radiate to the throat, upper jaw and left arm. Difficulty in breathing, sweating and dizziness may be experienced.

Lifestyle Adjustments (to reduce the effects of angina) Dietary and lifestyle changes can improve blood pressure control and decrease the risk of associated health complications:
• Eat a healthy diet – avoid junk food, sugar and salt, fried foods and saturated animal fats. Instead eat plenty of fresh fruit and vegetables, fibre and virgin olive oil.
• Give up smoking.
• Take regular, gentle physical exercise, for example a 20-minute walk daily, or a Tai Chi or yoga class.

Reflexology Treatment
• Heart area
• Lungs
• Diaphragm
• Solar plexus
• Adrenals

Heart: Pressure circles on cardiac area and circular massage:
- Press into a tender point for several seconds.
- Keeping this pressure constant, circle gently over the point several times.
- Deep pressure should NEVER be used on this area after a heart attack or if a pacemaker has been fitted.

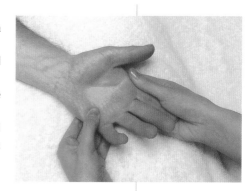

Lungs: Thumb-walk upper third of palm of hand (to the diaphragm line):
- Place the flat pad part of your thumb on the area to be treated, bend the first joint slightly and then unbend the thumb slightly so that you move forward a little. Continue in this way, moving forward in tiny creeping movements like a caterpillar, without losing contact with the hand.

Diaphragm: Pressure circles on the diaphragm line:
- Press into a tender point for several seconds.
- Keeping this pressure constant, circle gently over the point several times.

Respiratory Problems

Asthma

The causes of asthma are varied and include allergies such as pollen, house dust, fur, feathers, certain foods or pollutants. Stress often precipitates an attack.

Lifestyle Adjustments Asthma has no cure, but you can take an active role in managing the disease.
• Avoid dairy foods, which increase mucus production
• Yoga is very beneficial as it encourages deeper breathing as well as reducing stress
• Avoid irritating substances

Coughs and Colds

Reflexology is an excellent way of relieving the symptoms of the common cold and speeding up recovery time, but it is also remarkably effective at boosting the immune system. Regular reflexology greatly reduces the likelihood of catching a cold.

Lifestyle Adjustments Here are ways to boost your immune system so you can fight off coughs and colds:
• Eat garlic, which is 'nature's antibiotic'.
• Take at least one gram of vitamin C daily. Increase the dosage if you have a cold.
• Eat ginger, which helps to break down phlegm.

Nasal Problems

Nasal problems include acute or chronic catarrh, hay fever and sinusitis. Reflexology is renowned for its success with these problems. The most common causes are infections, allergies or the after-effects of a cold.

Lifestyle Adjustments Try either:
• Avoiding dairy foods, which encourage the production of mucus.
• Steam inhalation with the addition of essential oils such as eucalyptus and cajeput.

Asthma Reflexology Treatment

- Lung/chest area
- Solar plexus
- Diaphragm
- Adrenal glands for allergies

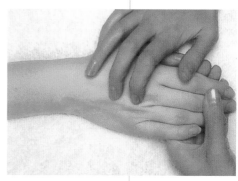

Lung/chest

Coughs and Colds Reflexology Treatment

- Lung/chest area – to break up the congestion and expel mucus
- Nose
- Throat
- Ears
- Eustachian tube
- Eyes
- Thymus – to boost the immune system
- Upper lymphatics

Nose

Nasal Problems Reflexology Treatment

- Face area
- Sinuses
- Adrenals – to counteract allergic responses
- Eyes and ears

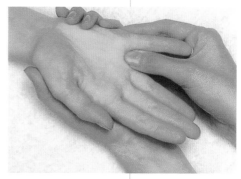

Sinuses

Skin Problems

Skin problems include acne, eczema and psoriasis and the causes are debatable. Hormonal imbalances, stress and certain foods appear to play a major part.

Lifestyle Adjustments (to treat and prevent skin problems) The skin reflects and reacts to imbalances within the body's internal landscape and the effects of the environment. Internal disharmonies caused by strong emotions, diet and your constitution, as well as environmental influences, all contribute to the development of a skin disorder. The following list may help to reduce your symptoms:

• Eat a healthy diet with plenty of fresh fruit and vegetables
• Drink six to eight glasses of water daily
• Avoid stress and learn to relax
• Avoid perfumed products. Use pure, organic skin creams

Reflexology Treatment
• Reflex zones relating to the areas of the body affected, e.g. face
• Pituitary gland – to balance the hormones
• Solar plexus – to relieve stress
• Adrenal glands – for stress and to counteract redness and itching
• Kidneys – to speed up elimination
• Lymphatics – to detoxify
• Digestive system – to encourage elimination

Face: Thumb- or finger-walk the front of the thumb:

- Place the flat pad part of your thumb or finger on the area to be treated, bend the first joint slightly and then unbend the thumb slightly so that you move forward a little.
- Continue in this way, moving forward in tiny creeping movements like a caterpillar, without losing contact with the hand.

Pituitary Gland: Hook-in and back–up on the centre of the thumb:

- Press your thumb into your chosen point and apply pressure (hook-in) and then pull back across the point (back-up).

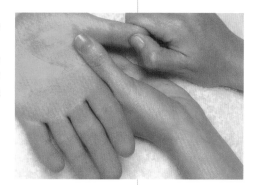

Treatments at a Glance

Foot Reflexology

Treatments at a Glance

When you have perfected your reflexology skills and are familiar with all the techniques you can use these charts as a quick reminder of all the treatments you need to know.

Both Feet
• Tuning in to the feet

Right Foot
Relaxation Techniques
• Effleurage/stroking
• Metatarsal kneading
• Alternate thumb rotations
• Zigzag spreading the foot
• Spinal stroking
• Spinal twist
• Toe-loosening
• Ankle rotations
• Foot-rocking

Step-by-Step Sequence
Tension release
• Solar plexus/diaphragm

Head and Neck Area

• **Head and brain** – thumb-walk back and sides of the big toe
• **Pituitary gland** – hook-in and back-up technique on centre of big toe
• **Face** – finger-walk front of big toe
• **Neck**
  – rotate big toe

– thumb-walk across base of big toe
– thumb-walk across front base of big toe
• **Sinuses** – walk down the centre and two sides of the small toes
• **Teeth** – finger walk down the fronts of the toes
• **Upper lymphatics** – gently squeeze the webbing between each of the toes
• **Spine** – caterpillar-walk down the inside of the foot. Repeat walking up the foot
• **Eyes and ears** – thumb-walk along the ridge at the base of toes. Press into eye point – between toes two and three, ear points between toes four and five.

Shoulder Girdle to Diaphragm Line

• **Thyroid, parathyroid, thymus** – thumb-walk ball of foot beneath big toe. Press thyroid point – centre of pad, parathyroid – over to the left slightly, thymus – right of thyroid gland
• **Right lung/chest** – thumb-walk chest area from diaphragm line to shoulder girdle line on sole of foot
• **Right breast/lung/mammary glands** – finger-walk front of foot from base of the toes to diaphragm line

Diaphragm Line to Waistline

- **Liver/gallbladder** – thumb-walk triangular liver area between diaphragm line and waistline. Rotate onto gallbladder
- **Stomach/pancreas/duodenum** – thumb-walk from inside of foot to approximately the centre of the foot
- **Right adrenal gland** – rotate adrenal gland

Below the Waistline

- **right kidney/ureter tube/bladder** – circle over kidney point, turn thumb and caterpillar-walk down towards inside of foot to bladder reflex
- **Small intestines** – thumb-walk from waistline to pelvic floor line
- **Ileocecal valve/ascending/transverse colons** – hook-in and back-up on ileocecal reflex, thumb-walk up ascending colon, rotate on hepatic flexure, thumb-walk across transverse colon
- **Right shoulder/arm/elbow/hand/hip/ knee/leg** – caterpillar-walk up and down outer edge of the foot
- **Sciatic nerve line/pelvic area** – thumb-walk down Achilles tendon area on inside of foot across hard heel pad and up Achilles tendon on outside of foot. Knuckle heel pad on sole of the foot
- **Uterus/prostate** – pressure circles with index finger on reflex points between inner ankle bone and tip of heel
- **Fallopian tube/vas deferens/lymph/groin** – thumb-walk inside of ankle, across the

top of foot to outside of ankle and back again
- **Right ovary/testicle** – pressure circles with index finger reflex located midway between outer ankle bone and tip of heel
- **Effleurage** – stroke right foot

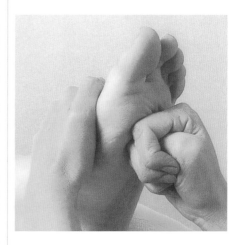

Left Foot

Relaxation Techniques

- Effleurage/stroking
- Metatarsal kneading
- Alternate thumb rotation
- Zigzag spreading the foot
- Spinal stroking
- Spinal twist
- Toe-loosening
- Ankle rotations
- Foot-rocking

Step-by-Step Sequence

Tension release

- Solar plexus/diaphragm

Head and Neck Area

- Head and brain – thumb-walk back and sides of big toe
- Pituitary gland – hook-in and back-up on centre of big toe
- Face – finger-walk front of big toe
- Neck
- – Rotate big toe
- – Thumb-walk across back of base of big toe
- – Thumb-walk across front of base of big toe
- Sinuses – walk down the centre and both sides of the small toes
- Teeth – finger-walk down the fronts of the toes
- Upper lymphatics – gently squeeze webbing between each of the toes
- Spine – caterpillar-walk down the inside of the foot. Repeat walking up the foot
- Eyes and ears – thumb-walk across ridge at base of toes. Press into eye point between toes two and three, ear point between toes four and five

Shoulder Girdle to Diaphragm Line

- **Thyroid/parathyroid, thymus** – thumb-walk pad between big toe. Press thyroid point – centre of big toe, parathyroid over to the right slightly, thymus – left of thyroid gland
- **Left lung/chest** – thumb-walk chest area on sole of foot from diaphragm line to shoulder girdle line
- **Left lung/breast/mammary glands** – finger-walk front of foot from base of toes to diaphragm line
- **Heart area** – thumb circles on upper third of sole of foot, index finger circles on top of foot

Diaphragm Line To Waistline

- **Stomach/pancreas/duodenum** – thumb-walk from the zone one to four from diaphragm line to waistline in horizontal rows
- **Spleen** – thumb walk from a zone five to zone four in horizontal rows
- **Left adrenal gland** – rotate onto gland

Below the Waistline

- **Left kidney/ureter tube/bladder** – circle over kidney area, turn thumb and caterpillar-walk to bladder area

- **Small intestines** – thumb-walk in horizontal rows from waistline to pelvic floor line
- **Transverse colon/descending colon/ Sigmoid colon** – thumb-walk across transverse colon, walk down descending colon (zone five), just before pelvic floor line turn thumb to the left until you reach sciatic line, circle over sigmoid colon, caterpillar-walk towards bladder area
- **Left shoulder/arm/elbow/hand/hip and/ knee/leg** – caterpillar-walk up and down outer edge of foot
- **Sciatic nerve line/pelvic area** – thumb-walk down Achilles tendon on inside of foot, across hard heel pad and up Achilles tendon on outside of foot. Knuckle heel pad on the sole of foot
- **Uterus/prostate** – pressure circles with index finger on reflex found midway between inner ankle bone and tip of heel
- **Fallopian tubes/vas deferens/lymph/ groin** – thumb-walk from inside of ankle, across the top of foot to outside of ankle and back again

- **Left ovary/testicle** – pressure circles with index finger on reflex located midway between outer ankle bone and tip of heel
- **Effleurage** – stroke left foot

Finale

- Return to any reflex points which were tender
- Perform any favourite relaxation techniques
- Run fingertips lightly over both feet
- Solar plexus release
- Cover up feet and allow receiver to relax
- Offer a glass of water and encourage receiver to drink plenty of water over next 24 hours

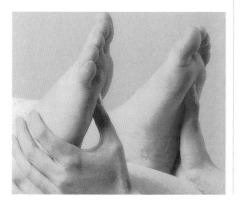

201

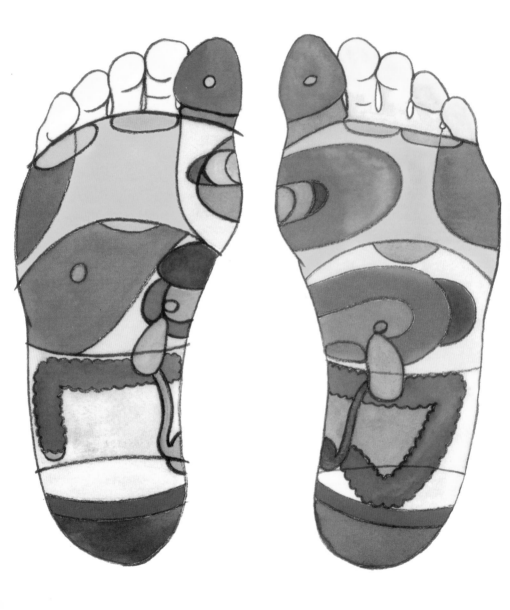

Detailed Foot Charts

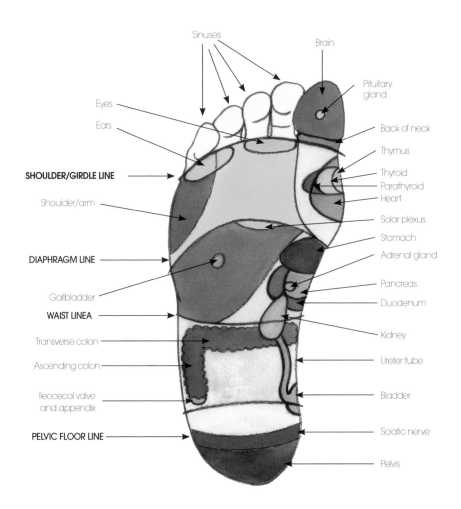

Sinuses

Brain

Eyes

Ears

Pituitary gland

Back of neck

Thymus

SHOULDER/GIRDLE LINE

Thyroid

Parathyroid

Shoulder/arm

Heart

Solar plexus

Stomach

DIAPHRAGM LINE

Adrenal gland

Pancreas

Gallbladder

Duodenum

WAIST LINEA

Kidney

Transverse colon

Ascending colon

Ureter tube

Ileocecal valve and appendix

Bladder

PELVIC FLOOR LINE

Sciatic nerve

Pelvis

Right Sole

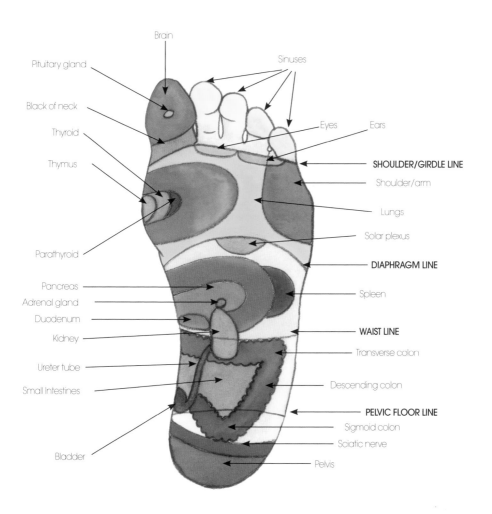

Brain

Pituitary gland

Sinuses

Black of neck

Thyroid

Eyes

Ears

Thymus

SHOULDER/GIRDLE LINE

Shoulder/arm

Lungs

Solar plexus

Parathyroid

DIAPHRAGM LINE

Pancreas

Spleen

Adrenal gland

Duodenum

WAIST LINE

Kidney

Transverse colon

Ureter tube

Descending colon

Small Intestines

PELVIC FLOOR LINE

Sigmoid colon

Sciatic nerve

Bladder

Pelvis

Left Sole

205

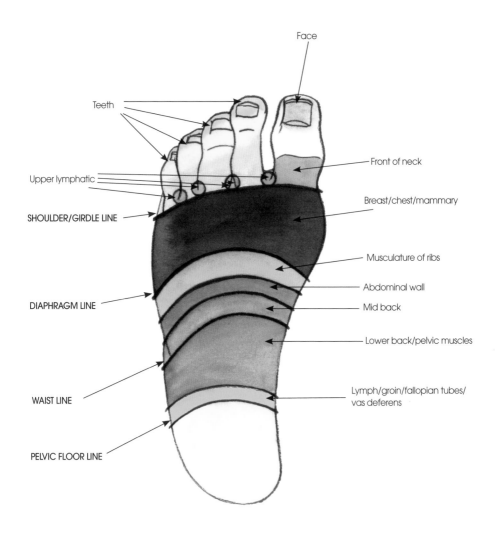

Face

Teeth

Front of neck

Upper lymphatic

Breast/chest/mammary

SHOULDER/GIRDLE LINE

Musculature of ribs

Abdominal wall

DIAPHRAGM LINE

Mid back

Lower back/pelvic muscles

Lymph/groin/fallopian tubes/
vas deferens

WAIST LINE

PELVIC FLOOR LINE

Dorsum – Left Foot

Outside View – Left Foot

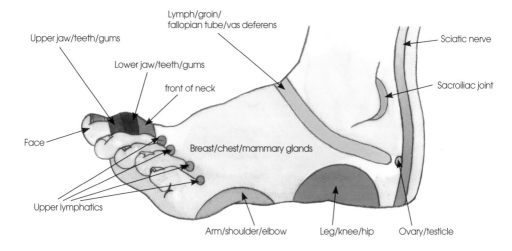

Lymph/groin/
fallopian tube/vas deferens

Sciatic nerve

Upper jaw/teeth/gums

Sacroiliac joint

Lower jaw/teeth/gums

front of neck

Face

Breast/chest/mammary glands

Upper lymphatics

Arm/shoulder/elbow

Leg/knee/hip

Ovary/testicle

Inside View – Left Foot

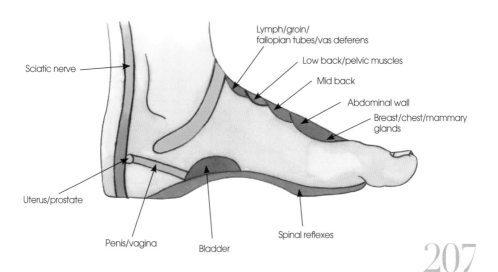

Lymph/groin/
fallopian tubes/vas deferens

Low back/pelvic muscles

Mid back

Sciatic nerve

Abdominal wall

Breast/chest/mammary
glands

Uterus/prostate

Penis/vagina

Bladder

Spinal reflexes

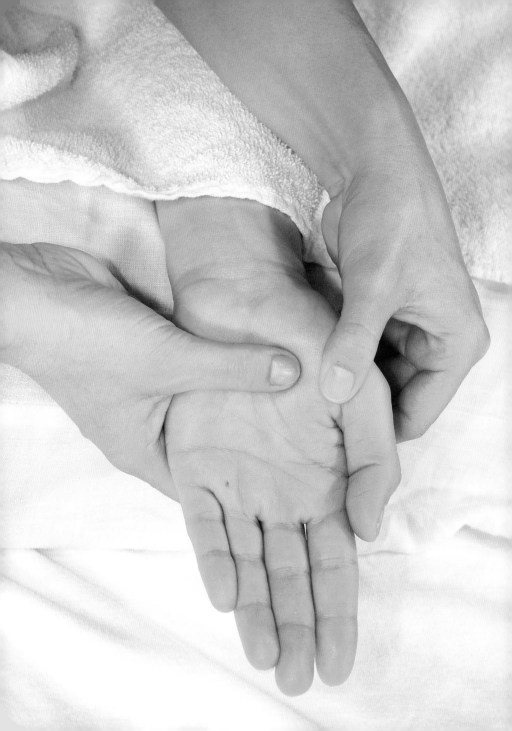

Treatments at a Glance

Hand Reflexology

Treatments at a Glance

Use the following pages to quickly keep track of the basic hand reflexology positions. They are an easy way to remind yourself of the movements while you are working.

Right Hand

Relaxation Techniques
- Greeting the hand
- Stroking hand and lower arm
- Stroking hand – palm up/palm down
- Opening the hand
- Knuckling the palm
- Loosening the wrist
- Moving the wrist
- Wrist rolling
- Loosening the fingers and thumb
- Moving the fingers and thumb
- Solar plexus release
- Fingertip stroking

Above the Waistline

- **Solar plexus/diaphragm**
- **Head and brain** – thumb-walk back and sides of thumb
- **Pituitary gland** – hook-in and back–up on centre of thumb
- **Face** – thumb or finger-walk front of thumb
- **Neck** – rotate base of thumb
- **Neck/thyroid** – thumb-walk across back of base of thumb
- **Neck/thyroid** – finger-walk across front of base of thumb
- **Sinuses** – walk down the back, sides and top of the fingers
- **Teeth** – walk down the front of the fingers
- **Upper lymphatics** – gently squeeze the webbing between each of the fingers
- **Spine/sciatic line** – caterpillar-walk down the inside (thumb side) of the hand (spine) and above the wrist (sciatic line)
- **Right eye and ear** – thumb-walk across ridge at base of fingers. Ear point (between fingers four and five); eustachian tube (between fingers three and four); eye point (between index and middle finger)
- **Right lung** – thumb-walk upper third of palm of hand (to diaphragm line)
- **Right lung/breast/mammary glands** – finger-walk down front of hand from base of fingers to diaphragm line
- **Liver/gallbladder** – thumb-walk zones five to three between diaphragm line and waistline. Hook-in and back-up technique on gallbladder reflex
- **Stomach/pancreas/duodenum** – thumb-walk zones one to three between diaphragm line and waistline

Below the Waistline

- **Right adrenal gland** – hook-in and back-up
- **Right kidney/ureter tube/bladder** – pressure circles over kidney point, turn thumb and walk down inside of hand to bladder.
- **Small intestines** – thumb-walk zones one-to-four
- **Ileocecal valve/ascending/transverse colon** – hook-in and back-up on ileocecal valve, walk up the ascending colon and across transverse colon
- **Joints right shoulder/elbow/hip/knee** – thumb-walk down outer edge of hand
- **Right ovary** – rotate on reflex point on outside of the wrist
- **Uterus/prostate** – rotate on reflex point on inside of wrist
- **Right fallopian tube/vas deferens/lymph nodes of groin** – thumb-walk across back and front of wrist
- Stroke right hand

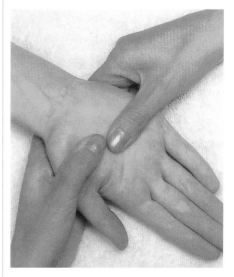

Left Hand

Relaxation Techniques

- Greeting the hand
- Stroking hand and lower arm
- Stroking hand – palm up/palm down
- Opening the hand
- Knuckling the palm
- Loosening the wrist
- Moving the wrist
- Wrist-rolling
- Loosening the fingers and thumb
- Moving the fingers and thumb
- Fingertip stroking
- Solar plexus release

Above the Waistline

- **Head and brain** – thumb walk back and sides of thumb
- **Pituitary gland** – hook in and back-up on centre of thumb
- **Face** – thumb/finger walk front of thumb
- **Neck** – rotate base of thumb
- **Neck/thyroid** – thumb-walk across back of base of thumb
- **Neck/thyroid** – walk across front of base of thumb
- **Sinuses** – walk down the back, sides and top of the fingers
- **Teeth** – walk down the front of the fingers
- **Upper lymphatics** – gently squeeze the webbing between each of the fingers
- **Spine/sciatic line** – caterpillar-walk down the inside (thumb side) of the hand (spine) and above the wrist (sciatic line)
- **Right eye and ear** – thumb-walk across ridge at base of fingers. Eye point (between

index and middle finger), eustachian tube (between fingers three and four), ear point (between fingers four and five).

- **Left lung** – thumb-walk upper third of palm of hand (to diaphragm line)
- **Left lung/breast/mammary glands** – finger walk down front of upper third of hand from base of fingers to diaphragm line
- **Heart area** – pressure circles on cardiac area and circular massage
- **Stomach/pancreas/duodenum** – thumb-walk zones one to three between diaphragm line and waistline
- **Spleen** – thumb-walk zones four to five
- **Left adrenal gland** – hook-in and back-up

Below the Waistline

- **Left kidney/ureter tube/bladder** – pressure circles over kidney point, turn thumb and work down towards inside of hand to bladder
- **Small intestines** – thumb-walk zones one to four
- **Transverse/descending/sigmoid colon/ rectum** – walk across waistline zones one to five, change hands to walk down descending colon, turn thumb 90 degrees to walk across sigmoid colon and into the rectum
- **Joints left shoulder/elbow/hip/ankle** – thumb-walk down outer edge of hand
- **Left ovary** – rotate on reflex point on outside of wrist
- **Uterus/prostate** – rotate on reflex point on inside of wrist
- **Left fallopian tube/vas deferens/lymph**

nodes of groin – thumb-walk across back and front of wrist
- Stroke left hand

Finale

- Return to any areas which were sensitive
- Perform any of your favourite relaxation techniques – use oil/cream if desired
- Run fingertips lightly over both hands
- Clasp both hands gently
- Cover up hands and allow the receiver to relax
- Offer a glass of water for and encourage receiver to drink six to eight glasses over the next 24 hours.

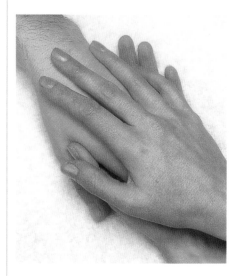

213

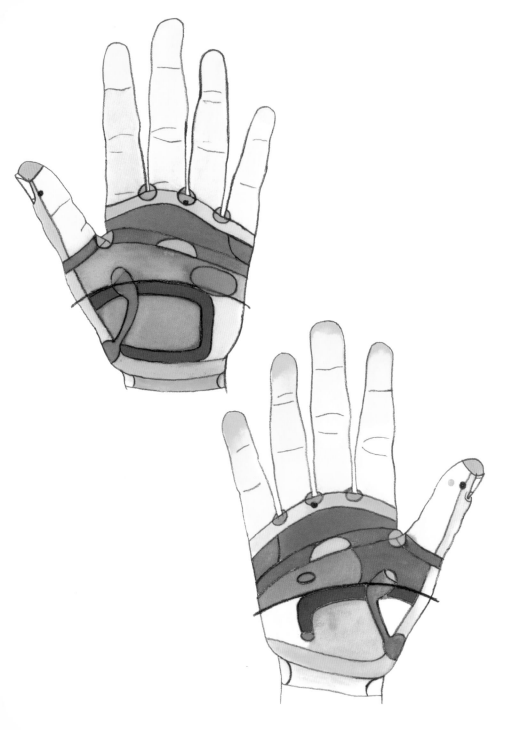

Detailed Hand Charts

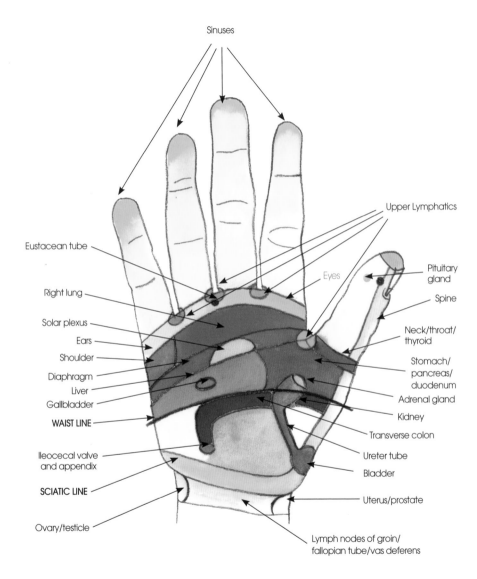

Sinuses

Upper Lymphatics

Eustacean tube

Eyes

Pituitary gland

Right lung

Spine

Solar plexus

Neck/throat/ thyroid

Ears

Shoulder

Stomach/ pancreas/ duodenum

Diaphragm

Liver

Adrenal gland

Gallbladder

Kidney

WAIST LINE

Transverse colon

Ileocecal valve and appendix

Ureter tube

SCIATIC LINE

Bladder

Ovary/testicle

Uterus/prostate

Lymph nodes of groin/ fallopian tube/vas deferens

216

Palm of Right Hand

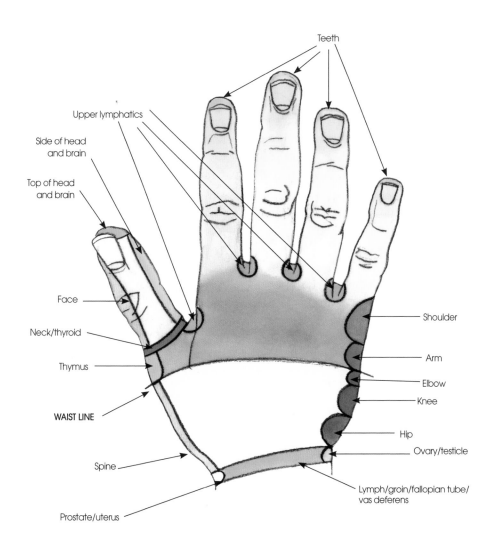

Teeth

Upper lymphatics

Side of head
and brain

Top of head
and brain

Face

Neck/thyroid

Thymus

WAIST LINE

Spine

Prostate/uterus

Shoulder

Arm

Elbow

Knee

Hip

Ovary/testicle

Lymph/groin/fallopian tube/
vas deferens

Back of Right Hand

217

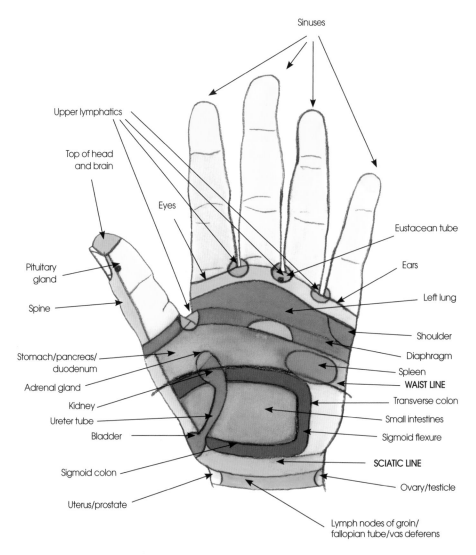

Sinuses

Upper lymphatics

Top of head
and brain

Eyes

Pituitary
gland

Spine

Stomach/pancreas/
duodenum

Adrenal gland

Kidney

Ureter tube

Bladder

Sigmoid colon

Uterus/prostate

Eustacean tube

Ears

Left lung

Shoulder

Diaphragm

Spleen

WAIST LINE

Transverse colon

Small intestines

Sigmoid flexure

SCIATIC LINE

Ovary/testicle

Lymph nodes of groin/
fallopian tube/vas deferens

Palm of Left Hand

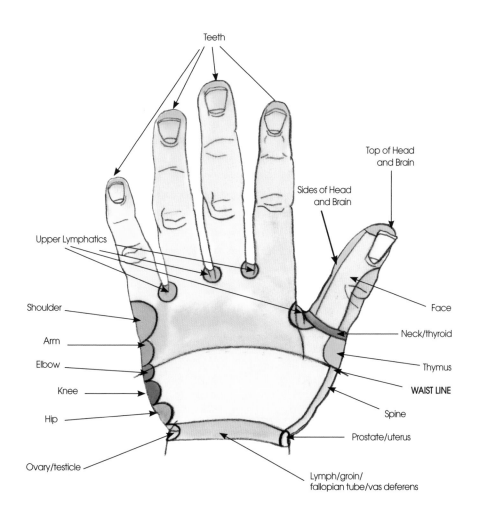

Teeth

Top of Head
and Brain

Sides of Head
and Brain

Upper Lymphatics

Face

Shoulder

Neck/thyroid

Arm

Thymus

Elbow

WAIST LINE

Knee

Spine

Hip

Prostate/uterus

Ovary/testicle

Lymph/groin/
fallopian tube/vas deferens

Back of Left Hand

219

Where to Go from Here

If you are receiving treatment from a practitioner or studying on a course yourself, be sure to check out the credentials available first. Here, we guide you through a few basic ground rules to follow.

Above A reputable reflexologist will provide a detailed consultation before commencing treatments.

Visiting a Reflexologist

Perhaps you would like to visit a professional reflexologist for a treatment. Check that your practitioner is fully qualified and insured rather than the product of a weekend workshop. Obviously the best way to choose a practitioner is by recommendation. Good practitioners are usually very busy, so be prepared to wait a while.

The initial consultation can take up to one-and-a-half hours. The reflexologist will take a detailed medical history and will also want to know about your lifestyle. Then your feet will be thoroughly examined for any imperfections that could indicate an imbalance in a reflex zone.

Then the treatment will begin and last approximately 30 to 45 minutes. At the end of the session you may be given self-help treatment to apply between sessions so that you can achieve faster results.

All in all it should be a very pleasurable experience. Patients usually feel very light and euphoric and have a warm glow all over the body. What a wonderful relaxing way to restore optimum health!

Advanced Training

Once you have practised and mastered the techniques in this book, you should have been encouraged by the results you have achieved while working on yourself, your family and friends. Hopefully reflexology is now an integral part of your daily life.

If this book has inspired you then you may decide that perhaps you would like to become a professional reflexologist. The image of reflexology has dramatically changed over the last 20 years. When it first began to be known in the West, during the 1980s, it was regarded with a good deal of suspicion and scepticism. Nowadays the field of reflexology is accepted and well-known all over the world. Now students regularly include doctors, nurses, osteopaths, chiropractors, physiotherapists and psychologists, as well as many lay people.

A recognised professional reflexology training will take at least nine months and will involve in-depth study in anatomy and physiology. The course should be accredited to a reputable reflexology association. Some schools simply issue their own certificates on completion of a course – these certificates can be worthless, expensive pieces of paper which are not recognised.

You should always check the qualifications of the principal. He/she should be a qualified teacher with at least five years clinical experience. Some individuals qualify and immediately set up their own courses without ever practising reflexology.

Never be afraid to ask questions if you are unsure about anything and perhaps arrange to go and see the college in action and look at the students' work and case histories.

Primary Reflexology Associations

UNITED STATES
International Institute of Reflexology
PO Box 12642, St Petersburg, FL,
33733-2642
www.reflexology-usa.net

Reflexology Association of America
2360 Corporate Circle, Suite 400,
Henderson, NV 89074-1122
www.reflexology-usa.org

UNITED KINGDOM
Beaumont College of Natural Medicine,
Unit 1 Heritage Courtyard, Sadlers
Street, Wells, BA5 2RR
www.beaumontcollege.co.uk

International Federation of
Reflexologists
London, EC3V 0BP
www.intfedreflexologists.org

CANADA
Reflexology Association of Canada
(RAC) Box 110, 541 Turnberry Street,
Brussels, Ontario NOG 1H0
www.reflexolog.org

AUSTRALIA
Reflexology Association of Australia
PO Box 253, Wynnum Central, QLD 4178
www.reflexology.org.au

If you are unsure, check with the main reflexology organizations in your region.

Index

Page numbers in **bold** refer to illustrations

Index